# FACING THE DARK:
# A Journey Into Suicide

## by Molly Ireland

Cover photograph by John Ireland
Cover artwork by Theresa Chipp
Cover design by http://vcbookcovers.com

ISBN  978-0-473-49918-1

Proofreading, editing, typesetting, printing and binding by
PublishMe, New Plymouth, New Zealand
www.publishme.co.nz

For Isabella, Chiara, Emma and Francesca, and to everyone else around the world who has lost someone they loved to suicide


In memory of Charles Edward Ireland
(11 June 1961–28 May 2008)


*"I am a forest and a night of dark trees: but he who is not afraid of my darkness, will find banks full of roses under my cypresses."*

- Friedrich Nietzsche, THUS SPAKE ZARATHUSTRA

## About The Author

Molly Ireland is a certified Neuro-Linguistic Programming (NLP) Master Practitioner, Instructor (NZANLP), Ericksonian hypnotist, and personal wellbeing coach (ICI). She specialises in the reduction of anxiety, depression and other mental health disorders and has helped thousands of families find hope and healing.

Molly trains New Zealand elementary, intermediate and secondary school teachers to better support students, and their families, at risk of depression and anxiety. She also works with people of all ages to transform depressive thinking styles and beliefs by helping them to re-write their personal and family "stories."

# Acknowledgements

I am on a journey that is not of my choosing but which, ultimately, has been to my benefit. During this time, I have tried to understand why my husband chose to embrace the darkness, while I was left to sustain the light for our four daughters and myself. *Facing The Dark* describes how I picked up the pieces to rebuild, and even, eventually, to rejoice in the new knowledge this journey has afforded me. There are many people I'd like to acknowledge for helping me reach this place of forgiveness and joy. They are truly remarkable human beings, whose unconditional support and love have made it possible for me to reach the point where I may share my story with you.

Firstly, I would not have gotten here without my four beautiful, now grown, daughters, Isabella, Chiara, Emma and Francesca. You gave me a reason to keep going through the toughest first years until I was strong enough to keep going for myself. I am eternally in awe of the amazing young women you've become. The loss of your father has and will continue to carve your "bowls".

I am truly grateful for the unwavering love and support of my husband, Francis, who has stood by my side and held my hand through many dark nights. He is truly a saint in human clothing for the way in which he helped me learn to trust and love again and for never giving up on me.

I'd like to thank my dear friends, Melissa Jordan, Jamie Scott and their sons, William and Jackson, for embracing the girls and me and becoming our first New Zealand family. But for your sheet-changing escapades, Friday pizza nights and late night singalong sessions, my journey would have been much darker. Without your "roll up your sleeves" approach, many hard times would have been unbearable.

I also want to acknowledge my dear friend and second mom, "Bunny," Virginia Heiner, whose grace and intelligence has always filled my spirit. I thank you for the endless hours spent editing my manuscript and for your tireless encouragement to keep going with this project.

I couldn't have gotten this far without my own family: my mother, Glenda, who's watching me from above, and my father, Ed, and stepmother, Theresa, with their boundless love. My sisters, Sadie, Rachel and Erica, and my brothers, Chuck and Keagan, for always encouraging me and making me laugh. To all of you, I just want to say I love you.

I would also like to acknowledge Charlie's mum and dad and Charlie's brothers, Bob and John, for their unconditional support, not only for the girls but for me, too, even during the worst of your own emotional pain. You truly are, and will always be, my English family.

I'd like to thank all my clients and their families who, over the years, have trusted and continue to trust me with their "stories" and struggles. I am so privileged to be able to help you reach for your own light during darkness and despair.

Finally, I'd like to thank myself for getting here. I know it may seem an odd thing to do, but this book was one of the hardest things I've ever done, for it required me to face my own darkness in a raw and tangible way. Releasing it out into the world signals the end of an era for me. I hope my story will help others hold the hearts of those they love and encourage everyone else to ask for help.

Molly Ireland
October 2019

# Contents

A Fleeting Moment

Dark Nights of the Soul

Overcoming My Fear of Wolves

Making Friends with the Dark

Navigating a Night Sea

A Prophetic Dream

Charlie's Family

My Father Was My Rock

Mom Knew from the Start

Dreaming Our Stories Alive

Our Tour de France

I'm Never Growing Old

Our Four Daughters

A Barometer

Surprise! We're Having Twins!

Looking for Love

A Broken Heart

The Stories We Tell

# Foreword

Suicide is fast becoming a national shame for New Zealand, with over 600 people taking their own lives annually. It is a serious social issue and barometer of the mental health of our population.

Each suicide casts a ripple, impacting on not only close family and friends, but also wider whanau and communities. Devastating, shattering, life-changing, traumatising are not too strong words to describe the effects of a suicide on those left behind. The cost is high emotionally, mentally, socially, and economically.

Molly Ireland tells the story of her grief process, broadly covering the facing and accepting of the reality of the loss and change that her husband's suicide brings about, working through the pain this has brought to her and her children, adjusting to life being different and re-investing in her new situation and finding ways to live positively in the future.

The community of suicide bereaved is one that no one wants to belong to and sets people on a journey of suffering, self-discovery, hard 'work' and growth. Through the pain and anguish something transformative can happen. Molly's therapist describes this as a carved bowl–"the deeper our suffering, the deeper we carve our bowls." She went on to say that the "carved bowl is invaluable because it gives depth to our souls and compassion to our hearts."

The Japanese have a form of art which they call "kintsugi",

in which they paint the cracks of a broken piece of pottery or china with gold, thus endowing it with a new kind of beauty.

While no one wants to embark on this journey of grief, part of making meaning out of a loved one's suicide includes finding benefits and the depth and compassion that Molly talks of certainly come into that category. While none of the benefits take away from the love for and loss of the person they do allow something positive to arise out of suffering.

Molly draws attention to the issue of suicide in our society. She rails against societal lies that imprison us and bend us out of shape to the point of seeing no other way out and offers another path, that of embarking on the road of personal growth, to discover our true selves and live in the joy of that.

**Heather Henare**
*Skylight Chief Executive*
*Kiwibank's Kiwi of the Year finalist (2017)*

*"I wanted only to live in accordance with the promptings which came from my true self. Why was that so very difficult?"*

- Excerpted from DEMIAN by Herman Hesse

# Prologue

I am an Alaskan living in New Zealand–a beautiful country with people who are kind, down-to-earth, generous and tolerant. I love this about Kiwis. They're a lot like Alaskans. I also love the bays, beaches, trees, ferns and native birds of this amazing place.

What I don't like is that so many suffer in silence from depression, anxiety and other forms of mental illness. So many "suicide," as they refer to it, taking their own lives. In fact, New Zealand has the highest youth suicide rate in the world, and few people talk about it.

After almost two decades of living with chronic depression, my husband and the father of my four daughters, Charles Ireland, or "Charlie," as we affectionately called him, died by his own hand on 27 May 2008.

Through this painful and devastating journey, I learned many things, including how to support people who are living the nightmare of either a personal depression or that of a suicidal loved one, and help them rebuild their lives.

Although the stigma and shame of suicide and depression

xiv

cast long shadows, there is a healthier way of relating to the darkness that lies within each of us so that it reflects our humanity and the eternal beings we truly are.

I hope my story will encourage you to face your own darkness and take the privilege of being alive to a deeper understanding in body, mind, and soul. I now know that we can overcome depression once and for all if we learn new ways of relating to ourselves. I know because I've done it.

When I was a teenager, my stepmother, Theresa, told me that we all have to "face our demons." We all have fears, difficulties to overcome, and heartbreaks that require enormous courage to conquer. I hope you will find in my words support and acknowledgment of your own "demons."

What I am about to tell you is absolutely true—every word. Writing this book was a painful experience, and yet I know I must tell my story if I am to live by Hesse's promptings. The telling of it involves a deep dive into both my failings and successes as a human being. I've told it because if you and I are to soften how we relate to depression and suicide, we must first look ourselves squarely in the face.

I do not mean to claim that every descent into depression is like my husband, Charlie's. His journey and mine are unique and very personal. I do hope, however, that you can awaken to the power of your own mind and the untruths you tell yourself. I also dearly hope that you, too, are able to find the courage to live by the promptings of your true self, regardless of how arduous this may be.

The promptings of my true self compelled me to write this for you, and I send it with great love and with the hope that your journey may be a little easier.

CHAPTER 1

# In the Beginning

*"Stars, hide your fires; let not light see my black and deep desires."*

- William Shakespeare, MACBETH

## A Fleeting Moment

When did I lose touch with the man I'd once promised to love and honour until death did us part? I wasn't sure. It happened gradually and yet came all at once. It took place right in front of my eyes, and I couldn't stop it. It became heavy, a swiftly moving, invincible force.

They say we can get used to anything. Now I know this to be true.

I'll never forget the autumnal Saturday afternoon in

mid-May when I sat on the bed looking at Charlie. Nothing about our new life felt right. I traced circles with my index finger on the duvet cover beneath me and felt as if I was facing the horrible reality of our predicament for the first time.

And then it happened.

Just for a split second as we sat there, deep love and acceptance for him filled my chest and spread through my being. An immeasurable sense of lightness and compassion came with it. For just a moment I wasn't trying to fix anything. I wasn't pushing him to heal. For a flash of an instant, I was able to see my husband as he was right then and right there in front of me. Not the way I wished he were– separate from his depression–nor within the fantasy of how I thought being married to him was supposed to turn out.

But as quickly as that loving lightness flooded through me, it withdrew and vanished from the room.

My girls needed me, I justified. I couldn't risk listening to his hopelessness as well as my own. I had to keep from falling down into that dark, deep hole, too. I had to keep at least one step ahead of my own gloom, otherwise the girls would have no one. With that, I went back to praying that another "good patch" was just around the corner.

## Dark Nights of the Soul

From an early age living in Alaska, I knew wilderness so dark that my hands disappeared in front of my face. I knew night skies so black that the heavens glowed in stark contrast against its palette—brilliantly, from millions of cosmic jewels.

North of Fairbanks, in Alaska's interior, the pink, orange and green waves of the Northern Lights dancing overhead were more like immense strobe lights at a galactic discotheque than the Aurora Borealis, and this is not an exaggeration. I am fortunate to know true darkness in this way because it brought me a sacred, celestial light. Most people today will never know the dark to the same degree, and I worry that we will have erased it from the planet before we become aware of its value.

Today, when we feel the closeness of nightfall, we quickly reach for a light switch. And just like our literal darkness, we attempt to chase away—with drugs and distractions, online or otherwise—the emotional darkness that lives inside us, too.

Literal and emotional darkness are equally vital to our humanity, asking that we turn inwards to be still and contemplate our lives, so we can question where we're going and for what purpose. Unfortunately, these "dark nights of the soul," as Thomas Moore calls them, can erode our essence if we do not embrace them, at least on some level.

If we try to extinguish the black lurking in our own shadows, then fear takes over and corrupts its alchemy. Ironically, our inner darkness becomes more entrenched, and we lose ourselves to the worry that we'll become stuck in it forever. Self-blame takes root and the shame that accompanies it is toxic.

## Overcoming My Fear of Wolves

As a seven-year-old, I faced my own darkness: an intrinsic fear of wolves. I'll never forget the day my mother announced I was to walk alone the half-mile from my family's log cabin to the bus stop for the first time. I begged her to drive me, but her response was a cool "No, Molly, it builds character."

From a young age, I knew the eerie, drawn-out howls of the Alaskan timber wolf intimately. My fiercely independent and hardy parents never seemed too concerned, but I was terrified. Once I overheard my father listening to the news as they talked about the low snowpack that winter. The lichen, usually nestled safely under blankets of packed snow, remained unprotected and exposed. The cold temperatures that year, even by Northern Alaskan standards, were excessive. As a result, the caribou and moose populations had dropped. This meant, according to the news announcer, that wolves were moving into more populated areas, killing domestic dogs as compensation. They had to eat, after all.

I remember thinking at the time that I wasn't much taller than my best friend's Siberian husky, Herman. My small size was a popular topic of conversation and ridicule for my peers. I'll never forget my second-grade teacher insisting that I stand next to the tallest boy in school so she could demonstrate our drastic height differences. My face flushed with embarrassment as my petite frame made its way to the front of the class. Not only was I about half his height, I felt at least half his age, also.

Roughly four hours of daylight were promised for my first solo trip to the bus stop but, unfortunately, not a single one of them could help get me there. The return trip would also have to be endured in the pitch black. That morning a deep dread consumed me as I got dressed and packed my lunch for school.

The temperature hovered close to negative 26 Celsius as I dressed in my usual gear: a calf-length goose down parka with matching lilac-coloured snow pants, face mask, wool scarf and wool mittens that were tucked inside a pair of black padded gloves. Finally, I slipped into my fluorescent pink Moon Boots, wishing Mom had bought the camouflage ones instead.

I glanced out of the living room window and, against a sea of black, I caught my small, heavily-clothed self in the reflection. As I overheard my mom say something to my little brother in the next room, I pushed open the front door, thrust myself out of the safety and warmth of our cabin, and forced myself into the abyss.

The icy air stung my cheeks. I blinked furiously trying to adjust my eyes to the dark, and even when I was able to make out the outline of the driveway in front of me, I continued blinking because I worried that if I didn't, my eyelashes would freeze to my face. With each crunch of snow underfoot and swish of my parka against my snow pants, I became more terrified. In my left pocket, I felt the flashlight Dad had given me for the trip, but I was too scared to use it.

By the time I'd made my way around the first bend in the road, less than 20 metres from our front door, my heart was pounding inside my head so hard that I half expected it to burst out. I scanned the snow banks on both sides as I continued my descent and every few seconds I looked behind me.

A levelling-off in the road meant that I'd made it to the first, and only, visible house en route. This was our only neighbour, and source of illumination, for at least 10 kilometres. That morning, the light shining from their kitchen window brought little relief when I thought about the owner's bite-sized Yorkshire terriers, Marla and Mercury.

I scaled the shadows of birch, aspen and white spruce trees that emerged from the forest and dominated the landscape. They seemed to stretch out forever into the endless dark.

Then, just as I neared the final forest clearing before the steepest part of the descent, I heard the howl of a distant wolf. Hurling my body forward, I broke into a panicked gallop that seriously tested my body's ability to cut through the icy air. It was another hour before my breathing relaxed after I took an empty seat on the bus to Fox Elementary School to start my first day of second grade.

In the days that followed, I tried different strategies to cope with the wolves lurking in the dark. There was the "run as fast as I can" approach, which only left me winded and feeling more terrified. Then I tried the "scan the snow banks with a flashlight on full beam" trot down the hill, which I hated even more than running. The flashlight felt like a devilish beacon announcing my intense vulnerability to the entire kingdom of canine predators. When I thought about the wolves' keen sense of smell, the "quick and sneaky" technique didn't provide any sense of security, either.

Eventually, I settled on the "silent but steady" strategy, which, except for the sound of my own breathing, was interrupted only by the sporadic outbursts of distant bellows. It took great concentration to stay with every "awww, woo, woo" that rose from their throats, to listen to the dips in decibels at the beginning of each cry, and to stay with the full throttle "woo, woo, woo" of the leader pushing his pack into song. The deep, mournful wail of a solitary male was the eeriest of all.

During the six years I walked alone to and from school, I never actually crossed paths with wolves, but I knew their entire repertoire of yelps, yips, barks, bellows, and howls as intimately as the sound of my mother's voice. I imagined their snouts lifted to the sky, and I felt each sorrowful wail vibrate in my chest. I made up stories about their lives, fantasies about their relationships, and explanations for their cries.

Sometimes, when the wolves' elongated howls seemed especially close, threatening to surround and overtake me completely, it took everything I had to stay true to my strategy. At those moments, I worked hard to listen to the silence beneath their howls.

The vulnerability these walks stirred in me was so primal that it forced me to deal with my fears head-on. Eventually, through this presence, I was able to make friends with the dark. And it changed my life.

## Making Friends with the Dark

As I drifted off to sleep one night, about eighteen months after my first solo walk to the bus stop, I remember thinking how regal the wolves were, and how lucky I was to know them. After that, I immersed myself in their long, drawn-out howls whenever I heard them. I soaked them in, and instead of being unsettling and scary, they became wild, beautiful and free.

Through this process, I began to relate to the dark in new ways. The literal darkness that played such a big part of my life became something solid and real, much more so than a simple absence of light. I could actually feel its heaviness on my skin as I breathed in time with it. The more I listened to the dark, the more it seemed to listen to me. Often, I couldn't tell where my body stopped, and it began. I felt as if I were floating, dissolving into space. With time, my eyes would narrow and de-focus as I adjusted to its shadows.

At the height of summer when it was never fully dark, and we were busy having barbecues or attending baseball games at midnight, I would actually miss it. As I entered adolescence, the darkness began to take on other meanings for me, too. It became a respite from my loneliness and an escape from the emotional chaos that the dissolution of my parents' marriage had brought to our family home. Surprisingly, when I felt alone and scared, the dark comforted me. It was in this way that I spent many long hours by myself.

Outside of school, because we lived so far from civilisation, I rarely saw other children my own age, particularly in winter when we were unable to leave the house for weeks at a time due to the heavy snowfall. This was how, when I wasn't doing chores or reading, the dark became my companion. I loved to walk in the spruce and birch forest that surrounded our cabin and large, dormant vegetable garden. It was then that I didn't just *feel* the dark, but I could smell and taste it, too. Beyond the frigidity of the air, dark air had a softer aroma and more tang to it than daylight. The dry, dark Alaskan winter air had a subtly temperate and less crisp odour and, strangely, it tasted earthy and almost briny as it slipped up my nostrils, moved over my tongue and along the roof of my mouth.

One evening when I was about nine, I was poking the snow with a stick at the rear of our cabin when I heard soft whimpers close by. Behind our dormant chicken coop I discovered a den at the base of a large pine tree. Peering inside I saw two pairs of shiny black eyes staring back at me; they were tiny wolf puppies yelping for attention! Quickly, I ran to get Mom, who was inside making dinner, and with flashlights in hand, we searched the area for signs that other wolves were nearby.

There were three pups in the litter, but only two were alive. Most likely, the other had starved to death, Mom said. The next morning, after reassuring ourselves that the mother wolf wasn't coming back, we carefully slipped the puppies out of their snowy den and relocated them to a large cardboard box by the wood burner in our living room.

For nearly six weeks, my brother and I cuddled and fed them with warm milk that we prepared twice a day. The smallest pup we called Flower and the bigger one, Moose. They were ravenous and grew rapidly before Mom found them new homes because, she said, "Wolves don't make good pets." I disagreed with her and said so, but she was adamant. I tried to tell her that I knew wolves differently after listening to their howls for so long.

I knew I could care for them, but I also knew that they were born to be free. So, one Saturday morning, after a family from the far end of Goldstream Valley came to collect them, I thought about how the dark had become a metaphorical friend, and then brought me literal ones, too.

## Navigating a Night Sea

My hands floated in front of my face, but I couldn't see them. Reaching into the dark, I tried to feel my way into knowing where I was: nothing. I ran my hands through the shag carpet and realised I was on the floor. At least I was still inside the house.

Extending my reach further, I finally felt a few clothes and a smooth, cool wall in front of me and on both sides. I slid my hands along the walls searching for a light switch, a door frame, anything to set me free from what felt like endless wall leading only to corners.

My hands continued their search, while my mind struggled to figure it out. I wasn't able to get past the walls, corners, and clothes. It was like a puzzle that should have been easy to solve, but I was disoriented, and, without the light, my eyes were of no use. I couldn't even see gradations of dark. I couldn't see anything. And this meant that I couldn't go anywhere.

I began to hyperventilate. How could I break free from this container that felt like a deep ocean or, maybe, the inside of a whale's mouth? Would I suffocate in this waterless sea of black? I awoke more fully and realised that I really couldn't escape from this giant cage, and I began to panic. When would this whale open his mouth? Where would this endless sea meet the beach? How could I free myself from this black abyss? Banging the floor and walls, I cried out, "Mooooooom!"

Suddenly, a light switched on and a door opened. Instantly, the night sea vanished, taking the whale with it. I was lying on the floor of my walk-in closet.

"What are you doing in here?" Mom asked, sharply. "You must have sleepwalked again," she said, without waiting for my answer. "Go back to bed. This is the third time you've done it this week!"

Slowly, I picked my eleven-year-old body off the floor and headed back to the safety of my bed. I was exhausted but unable to relax. I replayed the incident over and over again in my mind, wondering why most nights I journeyed to scary places. Just two days earlier, I had awoken to find myself curled up in the chair cavity of my desk, clutching a container of pens and pencils. Unfortunately, not all the dark places I've ventured to have been so benign.

At girl scout camp that same year, I was caught in the middle of the night trying to break into the locked armoury, where they kept the guns and ammunition stored for protection against bears. Apparently, I was trying to force the door open when a camp counsellor intervened. I figured out how I got there as he led me back to the cabin I shared with three other girls.

I was terrified to think that one night I might slumber outside during winter, only to freeze to death before I realised it. I dreaded falling asleep most nights. I started sleeping with a flashlight but, when I roamed, I never seemed to have it with me.

Through these experiences, I came to understand that we cannot make peace with the dark unless we have the light to see what it means in the first place. The dark is dark because we can't see it. This is what it is by definition. We have no awareness of it because we're asleep. It's hidden in our subconscious minds and we must shine a light, even if it is an unclear one. We must make it conscious so that it is no longer scary. We must wake up.

Mostly, the process of becoming conscious is preceded by fear, emotional pain, and sometimes panic—as I experienced many nights as a kid. But to benefit from the dark's potential, we must navigate the night sea that we all encounter from time to time, and dive in head first.

We must find a way to call out to the dark, asking to understand its motives, before we can soak up its gifts. I now understand that the best way to do this is to face the parts of ourselves we don't like and befriend them anyway. We must ask what these parts want from us, thank them for their promptings, and shower them with love.

## A Prophetic Dream

When I was ten years old, I had a dream that has stayed with me ever since. I rarely remember my dreams, but this one was too vivid to forget.

Standing outside a compound of buildings surrounded by a high barbed wire-topped fence and a gate locked with an enormous padlock, I glanced at a sign on the building in front of me: Movie Studio.

Aside from my family's annual Christmas viewing of *The Sound of Music* on TV, I had never actually seen a movie in a cinema. As I was thinking how interesting it was that people actually made films and that there were special places where they created them, a short, small-framed man with curly brown, shoulder-length hair and dark stubble emerged and spoke to me through the chain link fence.

"I can get you in here," he said, emphatically.

"Really?" I responded. "But what's your name?"

"Ireland," he said.

I will never forget these words. And it wasn't until I met Charlie, some fifteen years later, that I knew exactly why.

## Charlie's Family

Charlie grew up in St Albans, 41 kms north of London in Hertfordshire, England. He was the eldest son of a working-class London lad and a Southern Italian mum who was raised by an olive-farming family in Italy's Campania region. The family was structured and conservative, and it functioned on the sheer determination of a self-contained and disciplined Catholic mother. Quiet, reserved, and the quintessential martyr, his mom was nothing like mine.

My mom practiced martyrdom, too, but unlike his, whose strong faith in God allowed her servitude to her family to blossom underneath a protective barrier of stoic strength, my mom fought it with everything she had. She did so painfully, wearing it boldly on her lapel for the world to see. Both moms, however, spent most of their time in their respective kitchens expressing deep love for their families with food.

Our mothers also had their loneliness and isolation in common. Charlie's mom was in her late twenties when she emigrated to London and married Charlie's dad, five years her junior, bringing three sons into the world. Her whole life revolved around her boys. She didn't make English friends easily, nor did she try.

Charlie spent much of his early life keeping his mom company in the kitchen of their detached brick and tile home, about a fifteen-minute walk from the boys' school. Each afternoon when he got home, he'd sit down at the table next to the stove where she stood preparing the evening meal, and he stayed there long after mealtime was over, and the last dishes were put away.

Charlie was accommodating, just like me, which probably emerged from years of trying to soothe strong-willed mothers. Charlie's dad worked long hours as a sound editor in the film industry, often six days a week. Years later, a softness spread across her face as his mom told me how much Charlie's companionship meant to her. It was an important source of comfort for her during difficult times, she said.

After high school, Charlie headed north to study philosophy at Manchester University. Despite the degree, he neither enjoyed Manchester nor did he like university. He was capable academically, but his heart wasn't in it. University also stressed him out. He told me that, from an early age, he'd had a recurring dream that he was in the middle of exams and couldn't remember anything he'd learned; this wave of panic and anxiety seemed to follow him into adulthood.

He loved acting at Manchester, however. He even won acting awards, and his drama group won Student Play of the Year, which took them on tour across Europe. Charlie's dream was to be a stage actor in London's West

End, but he resigned himself to working behind the camera instead, when he missed out on one of the coveted places at London's Royal Academy of Dramatic Art (RADA). He only applied to RADA, when most people apply to at least three different schools, and when he didn't get in after applying only once, he took it very hard. He threw it all up in the air after one rejection.

There was a rigidity to his personality that latched onto perceived failures, stubbornly refusing to let them go, even as new opportunities and evidence to the contrary emerged. He mostly self-managed his disappointments by listening to melancholy music and riding his bike. He loved Morrissey. Not something Charlie grew out of after adolescence, Morrissey's music of despair became a key coping mechanism during difficult times.

Charlie's perceived failures bookended important decades of his life: the break-up with his first girlfriend when he was eighteen; his failed acting attempts at nineteen; the loss of film directing jobs in his thirties; and our departure from Hollywood in his forties. He framed each of these experiences as personal failures, and it never occurred to him that he could think of them differently. I witnessed this predisposition in him many times during the eighteen years we were together, and it seemed to worsen as his depression grew, or maybe as a result of it. I have no idea which, and neither, as far as I knew, did anyone else in his family.

What we all knew was that he was friendly and outgoing, personable and charming, someone who, despite his mother's tight apron strings, had many close friends. It was rare for anyone to take a dislike to Charlie after meeting him. People just loved to be around him.

He was very close to his brothers, particularly Robert, or Bob, the middle one. Bob always made Charlie laugh, and he adored him for this reason. John John, Charlie's baby brother, seemed to bring out the worst sort of grumpiness in Charlie, yet he loved him dearly and often said so.

Whenever we'd visit Charlie's family at home, he'd become sullen and moody. I always had the sense that he wished his parents were somehow different. A sense of frustration gripped him when we arrived and stayed with him until we left. Strangely, I got used to this and stopped being surprised by it. The thing that annoyed him the most was when his mom dumped large helpings of food on his plate without asking. Once, he stood up from the table with such force that his chair flew backward. His mom barely missed a beat, however, continuing to load his plate with large spoonfuls of gnocchi and vegetables.

"No!" Charlie shouted at the top of his lungs as he stormed out of the room. He found it difficult to say no to his mom, so when he did, it was usually with force. Mostly, though, he understood that this was just the way she showed her love for him–and love him she did.

I'll never forget the day we announced our plans to marry. Despite the fact that it was over a year away, his parents liked me, and Charlie was already in his early thirties, our news was received with a cold, stony stare. My soon-to-be mother-in-law was the first to break that silence in her strong Italian accent. "Dat is when I will be in Italy!" she stammered emphatically. "Soo I will noooooooot be coming!"

I stood up to leave the room when his dad muttered "Congratulations" meekly under his breath and I realised Charlie had nothing to say. I can only speculate on the reason for her reaction. My guess is that it brought up feelings she didn't want to face about losing her eldest son, and possibly this was made worse because I'm American.

Charlie's mom had lost many people she loved to my country of birth in post-WWII Italy. America had lured her siblings and cousins away with the promise of a better life than rural Italy could offer. Quietly, she hated America for this. I don't know for sure what was going on for Charlie's parents at that time, but I do know that they were uncomfortable talking about their feelings, and rarely did.

## My Father Was My Rock

I don't know when I stopped missing my dad. It wasn't a sudden thing, it just gradually diminished. Every Sunday afternoon, an emotional cocktail of sadness and fear had gripped me for as long as I could remember, and it wasn't until I was in my late twenties that I connected the dots.

My father, Ed, was a geologist and owned a mineral prospecting company, Resource Associates of Alaska (RAA). Monday through Saturday, year-round, he worked long hours, either at his office during winter, or out in the bush in summer. Sunday was the day he spent with us, and I looked forward to it like most kids long for Christmas.

My dad was my grounding rod. He was playful, intelligent and—most of all—calm, and I felt the same when I was with him.

Dad was a relief from the turmoil of living with Mom. My times with him were too short, and the anticipation of Sunday evenings, after which I would have to wait at least another week to see him again, was awful. Every Sunday my stomach ached with that familiar sense of dread. It was as if a burlap bag laden with cement had been thrown over my head.

My mother, Glenda, was the disciplinarian. She doled out the wooden spoon for all sorts of misdemeanours, both trivial and significant alike. I'll never forget the exact layout of our laundry room (the Punishment Room) where we awaited the spoon. My mother's industrial sewing machine dominated the far corner, piles of books lined the walls on either side, and the double-decker washer/dryer hid behind the door.

I knew the curve of the washing machine window door intimately after tracing it with my finger many times. That was where I waited until she was ready to punish me. Those times seemed like the freeze just before the thaw, when that first trickle of moisture begins to seep very slowly from the ice, steadily and unrelentingly pushing its way to the surface to crack the hardened mass and release its hidden liquid.

My backside felt cracked, too, after a spooning, which was usually as a result of some snarky comment I'd made. Nobody ever confronted my mother. I eventually learned there was no point in trying, although I'm not sure my brother ever did.

Mom ruled our house as if she had an iron grip around the neck of a turbulent tornado. She was rarely at peace unless she was cooking. Mostly, she was in turmoil, emotionally unstable, and terrifying in her seemingly instantaneous mood swings. As a kid, I watched her like a herd of caribou watches the wolves on the tundra, continuously and from a distance. And yet, she was also incredibly loving.

I knew she loved us with all her heart. She worked hard to be the perfect mother, and that was the problem. She tried too hard. Instead of relaxing into her maternal intuitions, she forced her motherhood onto us from a place of deep insecurity. We had to be hard-working, musically talented and well-presented at all times. These standards were as exhausting for her as they were for us. To live them every day required a sheer force of will that required her to take daily afternoon naps to maintain.

It was during her nap time that my brother and I would let loose, and we always did so very quietly.

## Mom Knew from the Start

It was Mom who told me about Charlie's depression. I hadn't noticed it before or, more accurately, had no way of recognising it, and I dismissed her at the time. She was, after all, my overly-involved and often intrusive mother, even when I became an adult and had a family of my own.

Mom was also annoyingly perceptive and blunt at times. One visit, as she was finishing her Master's in psychology, she announced at the breakfast table that she had decided to give her future son-in-law a "psych test" before we married later on in the year.

Mom was difficult to contradict. I have spent a lifetime trying to establish strong personal boundaries that allow me to walk into a department store, try something on, and hear my own opinion about the outfit, and not just hers.

As a child, I adored spending time with her in the kitchen, watching as she added each ingredient into the dish we were preparing. Thanksgiving was her favourite day of the year because it revolved around meal preparation. Each year she would try to make her turkey even more succulent than the last, as if she were the only contestant on *My Kitchen Rules*. My sister, Sadie, and I would spend hours helping her fix those feasts—and feasts they were—talking and laughing together, with little else to distract us.

Mom also loved the Alaskan night sky. Some of my fondest memories with her were the times we cuddled together, all rugged up against the cold, to gaze in wonder at the stars and Northern Lights. My grandfather walled-in and insulated our viewing deck for that purpose. I loved when the Northern Lights would waltz and shimmy overhead for us as if it were our personal, magical light show. The heaviness of our lives and mom's accompanying emotional pain dissipated with each celestial sway, and I felt loved and especially close to her.

As the eldest child, Charlie, too, had difficulty filtering

out the voices and opinions of everyone around him, especially those he loved the most. I can still see him sitting at the kitchen table that morning, patiently filling out Mom's questionnaire while she hovered in the kitchen nearby, ready and overly eager to proclaim his suitability as my husband.

The only thing I remember after Charlie handed the form back to her, however, was the silence. Usually, Mom gave us a running commentary on just about everything–the significant and trivial alike. But she didn't say a word as she reviewed his psych test results. When she looked up and saw us staring at her in anticipation, she just muttered under her breath that she needed to ask her professor about it and set the papers aside.

Despite the strangeness of this event (my mom was not a mutterer), I didn't spend much time thinking about it. In fact, I was grateful she hadn't made a big deal out of anything so we could get back to enjoying her visit.

Mom was just herself: hard-working, determined, outspoken and loving. Years later, I overheard her talking to our piano teacher after he had driven fifteen miles from East LA to our house in Topanga Canyon to give Isabella her weekly lesson. I was stunned to hear her say, "You must be single, am I right? You don't have a lot going on in your life to drive all the way out here just to give a piano lesson to a six-year-old?" It was no surprise that we didn't see that piano teacher ever again. That was my mom. She said it like it was or, at least, how it was for her.

Despite her abrupt approach and strong outer persona,

she, too, suffered from bouts of depression that I knew nothing about until much later. It's strange how you can think you know people, particularly those really close to you, and yet each of us, ultimately, is a stranger. We really have no idea what goes on in someone else's head. Just like my impressions of Charlie, I thought I knew what made my mother tick, yet these thoughts were only stories I told myself about her.

Mom tried to bring up the results of Charlie's psych test a number of times after she returned to America with my stepfather, Jim, but I didn't really listen. When she said he had depression indicators, I thought she was talking about his occasional moodiness and tendency towards binge eating. I thought I knew what she meant. I wasn't ready or able to face the darkness that was coming to us both.

> *"Every human is an artist. And this is the main art that we have: the creation of our story."*
>
> - Don Miguel Ruiz

## Dreaming Our Stories Alive

According to the ancient Toltec wisdom of Mexico, the world is a dream, and we are always dreaming it into existence. I dream my dream and you dream yours, and together we create the dream of our planet. Everything I believe is filtered through my dream, or what can be called my story.

Throughout my life, the telling of my story is how I speak it into existence. Through repeated performances, I lay down neural pathways that are measurable on brain scans. This is how I practice my story, and it becomes written.

We all believe that our dream is the only accurate way to explain "reality." The truth is that my dream is only mine, not yours, even if there are places where our dreams intersect. We think our story is the one, true tale, and we default to autopilot, becoming stuck on a single interpretation; the one we have grown accustomed to, or seen modelled by the people we love.

When we forget that our story is just a dream, we become incarcerated by its plot line, believing that we have no control over its twists and turns. We don't realise that many re-writes are possible, if only we dare to re-imagine them. Alternate versions, and very different outcomes and endings, can be created if we choose to re-write the familiar.

In telling you my story, along with its revisions, I hope I can inspire you to re-write your own story and wake up from your personal dream.

In making sense of our world, our stories can inspire or insult us. Too often, unfortunately, they spread lies about our integrity and self-worth. Charlie's life is testimony to what can happen if we repeatedly and unconsciously practice a very dark dream. I only wish he could have realised it.

## CHAPTER 2

# Early Days with Charlie

*"Everyone is a moon and has a dark side which he
never shows to anybody."*

- Mark Twain

## Our Tour de France

After meeting at a mutual friend's birthday barbecue in Brixton, London, in the summer of 1991, Charlie and I married in Vancouver, Washington, on 24 July 1993. Surrounded by family and friends from both England and the United States, we enjoyed a wedding reception among the giant hydrangeas on the banks of the Columbia River, just outside Portland, Oregon. Afterwards, we spent a few days recovering in the Columbia River Gorge before returning to London so Charlie could finish up his work on Mark Herman's comedy film, *Blame It on the Bellboy.*

Two years later, after relocating to Los Angeles so that Charlie could pursue a film career in Hollywood, our first daughter, Isabella Irene, was born. As much as Charlie loved film making, he loved road cycling even more. So, when Isabella was about eighteen months old, and we'd recovered from the shock of becoming new parents, we set off on a cycling adventure: our own Tour de France, he called it.

The three of us embarked on a six-week-long trip along the Pacific Coast Highway (PCH) from my mother's house just outside Portland, Oregon to my dad's house in Gardnerville, Nevada, near Lake Tahoe. I loved every one of those 1,200 miles we ventured, mostly in sixty to seventy-mile chunks. Charlie pedalled religiously for up to ten hours a day, while Bella and I followed along in the car, playing support crew and taking in the sights.

Each morning after breakfast, Charlie would get into his cycling gear and head off to our designated meeting place for lunch. Leisurely, I would pack up the car while Bella played alongside me.

It felt like a grand adventure: planning each day's journey by flashlight in the tent the night before, sharing tales of the interesting people and critters we'd seen and, most of all, the songs Bella and I made up along the way to share with Charlie each night by the campfire. It was a magical time with plenty of laughs.

Overlooking the majestic Pacific Ocean from our

campground just outside Mendocino, California, I'll never forget the morning Charlie pulled himself into his tight Lycra cycling shorts after rubbing mentholated Deep Heat onto his thighs to ease the muscle pain. I looked up from washing the breakfast dishes at the nearby tap to see him furiously hopping around the campfire on one foot, howling in pain. Without realising the implications, he'd managed to drag the menthol ointment across his sensitive nether regions. Callously, Isabella and I would laugh about it on and off for the rest of that trip and many years thereafter.

## I'm Never Growing Old

I felt a deep sense of pride in Charlie when we finished that cycling road trip together. Riding through all kinds of weather, with severe saddle rash, near misses with raccoons and coyotes, and all kinds of physical pain, he had done it. Even though he never said so, I assumed that he too must have felt some sense of accomplishment. He never spent much time thinking about what he'd achieved, however. Most of our married lives together he amplified what he saw to be his faults and failures, rather than his successes.

I remember one conversation with him that puzzled me at the time.

"Our next cycling road trip should be from your parents' house in Hertfordshire, England, to their olive grove in Southern Italy," I suggested to him on the last morning of the "Tour" after leaving the Sierra Nevada Mountains to head into the Truckee Meadows, just outside Reno.

"That would be great," he responded, encouragingly.

"It will just have to be before we get too old and too sore," I teased, ruffling his mop of dark curls.

After a few moments' pause, he continued, "I'm never going to grow old, Molly. So, we'd better do it soon."

I thought this was a strange way to look at things, a bit ridiculous even. Of course everyone grows old.

## Our Four Daughters

Our daughters have always been an anchor and a great source of happiness for us both. Despite the stress and strain of having four kids in six years, Charlie loved Isabella, Chiara, Emma and Francesca with everything he had. He called them "my girls."

During good patches, he played the Beatles' *Rubber Soul* LP loudly, picking up each girl in turn, holding her close to his chest as they both swayed and jiggled to the music.

God, I loved those days. I can remember sitting on the sofa watching him purposefully line up the girls so that each daughter knew whose turn it was next. When Emma started to wiggle out of her place in line from excitement, he'd glance over at her and she'd scuttle back into position. I'll never forget the look on their faces as each girl awaited her turn to dance with Daddy!

"Michelle, maaaaa belle..." we would all sing at the tops of our voices, and up, up, up in the air Chiara would go flying before he caught her in his arms and set her back down again, grinning from ear to ear. Those times never seemed to last long enough, and at some point, they were behind us.

Unfortunately, Charlie left his dancing days in LA, along with his dream of being a film director.

## A Barometer

Every morning for as long as I'd known Charlie, he made me a cup of coffee. No ordinary coffee, mind you; it was a deliciously creamy cappuccino made with great care and attention. In fact, the eventual cup I enjoyed was somewhat of a masterpiece, the only survivor in a line of throwaways. Everything from the hardness of the water, the coarseness of the grind, the pressure of the stack, and temperature of the cup and milk, had to be just right at each step of the way. Otherwise, at some point in the process, it was considered a failure and thrown down the sink.

Depending on his mood that day, my morning cup could have been number two or three if the day started well, and he was looking forward to a long cycle ride later or, possibly, number five or six if he hadn't slept well and had no job prospects at the time.

Charlie owned a better espresso machine than do most small cafés in New Zealand. It was a beautifully crafted piece of Italian machinery made from high-grade steel and covered in polished chrome. Weighing nearly 33 kgs, it was nearly the same size as my first car and, definitely, cost more.

Making coffee was mostly a manual process for Charlie to maximise his professional grade machine's vacuum brewing process. When we left LA, he had the machine gutted and re-wired to operate on New Zealand's 220 electric volts.

Charlie loved making coffee for everyone who came around, day or night. It was an art few people could replicate. His exacting standards may have started with making cappuccinos but extended to everything else he did, too. This made him great to work with but difficult to be married to. He was particularly hard on himself when he couldn't live up to these high standards, and the only explanation for not meeting them was to label them failures and toss them down the sink.

## Surprise! We're Having Twins!

In June of 2001, we received the biggest shock of our lives.

Isabella was nearly six, and our second daughter, Chiara Amelia, hadn't yet turned three. I was due to have our third baby that August. My extremely wise and seasoned nurse midwife, Nancy, had been pestering me for most of my pregnancy to get an ultrasound because my measurements were so out of whack that she was certain my dates were wrong. I knew they were correct; I just thought we were finally having a big boy!

Busy with the two girls and working full-time, I postponed and rescheduled the visit to the obstetrician for as long as was feasibly possible—until six weeks before my due date. It wasn't until Nancy told me that if I didn't do it she wouldn't deliver this baby that I finally took action.

I have always disliked medical procedures of any kind, which was why I'd chosen to have Isabella and Chiara at the Natural Childbirth Centre in Culver City with Nancy. This time I had even rented a water birthing tub, which was scheduled to arrive in three weeks' time. I was determined to have my last baby at home.

And then we met Dr. David Kline. Stand-up-comedian-turned-obstetrician-gynaecologist, he had the bedside manner of Mother Theresa, despite his showbiz credentials and mid-town LA location. From the moment Charlie, Chiara and I showed up in his ultrasound room that Wednesday morning in late June 2001, I was at ease. We'd decided to keep Chiara out of preschool that day so we could have breakfast at the café around the corner afterwards.

Pulling out a measuring tape and extending it over my stomach, he said, "Oh, yes, you are rather large. Let's just take a look here."

Lubricant in hand, he squirted a big dollop of gel onto my swollen stomach. Feeling relaxed and excited for my first glimpse of our new baby, I glanced at Charlie standing at the foot of the table. He looked eager to get a peek, too. Totally absorbed by the toys the nurse had just handed her, Chiara was sitting on the floor, playing.

"Oh, yes, I see." Sliding the hand-held device all around my abdomen, Dr. Kline calmly pronounced, "There's more than one in here!"

"What?" I gasped in shock. "What do you mean more than one?"

The room went silent. My brain went black.

"Yes, the reason you're so large is that you're having twins. Wait..." he paused. "Let's just check to make sure there's not another one hiding in here!"

"What?!" I shrieked, as Dr. Kline continued his search. When I looked at Charlie, he was pale as a ghost and was starting to drop to his knees.

"No, no, just twins," the doctor reassured.

"That can't be, twins don't run in our family!"

Charlie was gone from my sight. I was hoping he hadn't passed out and was just sitting with Chiara on the floor. A stream of questions poured out of my mouth, sounding more like a cross-examination.

"Are they alive? Are they attached?" I demanded, envisioning an interconnected mass of tissue. "Are you sure? Let me see."

I imagined all the different configurations of Siamese twins I had seen many years before in my high school biology textbook.

For the next hour, Dr. Kline patiently reassured us that everything would be okay as we deciphered the ultrasound images flashing in front of us. Our shock and dismay at the news of doubling our number of children overnight, and learning this fact so late in my pregnancy, prompted the doctor to calmly say to me as we prepared to leave his office, "This is why women have early ultrasounds, Molly."

## Looking for Love

For as long as I can remember, I have always wanted to be loved. Not that this is unusual; humans are programmed to seek it out. And yet, for me, it was extreme, off-kilter and out of balance. For almost fifteen years, I had the same dream. I loved a man who didn't love me in return. Sometimes that man was my father, but mostly it was a romantic partner I didn't recognise, and whose love I longed for, yet never secured. Different settings, different men, but always the same outcome: I loved him, and he didn't reciprocate. It wasn't that he was unkind or anything, he just didn't care.

And this broke my heart.

In 1998, at our house in Sherman Oaks, in LA's San Fernando Valley, shortly after our second daughter, Chiara Amelia, was born, I remember having a conversation with Charlie that made me reflect on this dream and wonder about the ways in which we make up stories.

We were sitting outside in the warm night air after the girls had gone to sleep, enjoying a glass of Cabernet Sauvignon together in one of those rare parenting moments of peace. That night our neighbourhood was graced by an anonymous bagpiper, who often practiced his haunting Scottish melodies when the sun went down. I remember feeling serene as his mesmerising music worked its way over the Hollywood Hills and down into our backyard.

I had been doing some soul searching after Chiara was born because my doctor told me that I, too, had become depressed during my postnatal recovery. Chiara was only a few months old, and I was weighing the pros and cons of taking antidepressants while I was still breastfeeding.

Out of the blue, I said, "You know, Charlie, I haven't listened to you very well in the past and I'd like to change this now. I really want our relationship to be stronger."

There was a long, uncomfortable silence. Okay, now it's your turn to talk, I thought. The seconds ticked by, and I reminded myself just to wait. I'll never forget what he said next because it knocked me to my knees. "I don't love you," he said. "I never have. You forced me to marry you, and I just went along with it."

My vision went black and my throat tightened. My mouth gaped open, but nothing came out. His words slammed into my stomach; I was too stunned to breathe.

For months afterwards, all I could think of was how

my recurrent dream had actually come true. Here I was in love with a man who didn't love me back.

There it was, plain and simple, out in the open for me to face. My absolute worst fear had manifested itself, and an understanding of it would only come from living with it.

## A Broken Heart

The moment Charlie told me he didn't love me would come to define our marriage for me. It also formed the basis of a personal story I created based on denial and resignation. For all my obsessing over the consequences of that conversation, I hadn't realised how much I'd hollowed myself out as a result of it.

Gradually, I came to figure out that I had to pretend it didn't matter if he loved me or not. If I was going to survive and keep my family intact, I would have to carry on as if he'd never said it. At first, I worked hard to believe this until eventually it became my truth and I was able to tell myself that it didn't matter either way.

Sometimes I pretended that he did love me deep inside, but he just couldn't find it. For other people, I pretended that we were happily married, and I also pretended that everything would change as time went on. But mostly, I checked out. I began making light of his dark moods when a director wouldn't call about a job, or when he'd just finished off a two-litre tub of mango sorbet while watching a half-hour sitcom on TV.

Charlie stopped sleeping in our bed, and I started planning family vacations that I knew he wouldn't attend. I took the girls to see my family more often and carried on working and trying to raise my daughters as best I could.

In this way, I kept going and focused on the aspects of my life that I could control. A huge, hollow cavity imploded into my chest, which I only noticed when he would, occasionally and out of the blue, reach for me.

> *"What hurts you, blesses you. Darkness is your candle."*
>
> - Rumi

## The Stories We Tell

We are simultaneously the author of our stories and the characters within. We have the ability to create wholeness and love, or destruction and death. Everything I see, hear, and feel, I expected first in my mind, and then it came into being. This is why we are such phenomenal creators, and this ability to imagine gives us tremendous power and responsibility. But, mostly, we are unaware of it.

Asleep, we are lost in the mist. We can't see what is right in front of us. We try to speed through the dense fog of our own creation and wonder why we can't find any way out. We wonder why we go in circles, recreating what we don't want, and then acting destructively, mostly to ourselves. Until we slow down and shine a bright light on the forces hard at work creating our life stories, we won't get anywhere. We will continue to be lost in the fog.

Our thoughts, feelings, and beliefs work tirelessly behind the scenes to form the foundation of our personal stories.

Our thoughts become the narrators of our stories by giving birth to our inner voices. They tell us what they think is coming next, and the supposed meaning of what's already happened. "You won't get that job," your thoughts tell you, "because you were overlooked last time." "He won't go out with you," your thoughts continue. "He's too gorgeous for the likes of you." Your thoughts also give you advice: "Don't ask her out because you might make a fool of yourself." If left unchecked, your thoughts narrate a dark and depressing story, morphing into critical tyrants who assault you day and night.

If our thoughts are the narrators, then our feelings and emotions become the characters who interact with one another to make our stories interesting. Our stories contain many characters who conform to the roles we play on any given day. The loving parent, for example, is created by our nurturing and empathic feelings for our children. There is also the controlling critic, who is always trying to make us better but is fed by our fears and insecurities; the inner marketing manager, who invents sales pitches out of feelings of stress and ambition; and the impulsive shopper born out of a sense of impatience and entitlement. We may also recognise our frustration in the naughty two-year-old who sometimes throws temper tantrums, and toys from the crib.

Regardless of which characters your story features, it's driven by strong personalities and, if left unchecked, these characters will sabotage your re-writes, especially if you try to script them out of your plot-line altogether. Before we can ask our emotions, and the characters they play, to step away, we must first listen to, and befriend, them. We must understand that they're only trying to help us but are going about it in dysfunctional and ineffectual ways.

Our thoughts and feelings flesh out our stories, but it's our beliefs that are foundational to how our stories unfold and where they'll end up. Beliefs form the structure of our stories because they're born from thoughts and feelings that have hardened over time. They're not "hunches" any longer; there's so-called "evidence" or proof that they are, indeed, true.

Because of this, our beliefs are good indicators of how our personal plot lines will unfold: what we will and will not experience in our lives. If we believe, for example, that we're unlovable then we will long for a love that we can't find, and people will reject us. If we believe we aren't talented enough, we'll cry out for recognition and be overlooked for promotions. If we believe that our efforts usually end up as failures, we'll create opportunities to screw up and make more than our fair share of mistakes.

Only when our original drafts don't turn out the way we expected them to can we begin to explore the thoughts, feelings, and beliefs that underpin them. It's easier, however, to live our life stories on autopilot without questioning what we do or considering other possibilities and options.

When, one day, something happens that shakes us to the core (or we become ill from the exhaustion of racing blindly around in the fog for so long) we can finally understand that we must wake up and revise our stories or self-destruct.

At these critical life junctions, we make a choice to live or die. Even if we don't realise that we've chosen to die gradually over a long time—rather than by our own hands all at once—the outcome is still the same: death.

# CHAPTER 3

# Finding Help

*"We are all prisoners but some of us are in cells with windows and some without."*

- Khalil Gibran

## A Fractured Skull

Jerking awake, I reached for the ringing phone. The clock read 1:45 a.m.

"Hello. Charlie, is that you?" I said, attempting to make out the garbled sound of his voice. "Are you okay? Talk to me. What's happened?" There was a long pause, and then I heard him slowly and deliberately struggling to form words.

"I'mmmm hurt," he stammered.

"What?" I asked. "Are you drunk? Where are you?"

"I'm, um, in Calybaaaasez," he responded, taking shallow gulps of air and trying to communicate with me. "I'mmm, um... blood."

"I'm on my way to get you now. Where are you?" I demanded. "Tell me exactly where you are."

Then the phone went dead. I dialled his cell phone several times, but it cut straight to voicemail. My heart raced. What was I going to do now? How was I going to find him? I hastily threw on a cardigan and sweatpants, grabbed the keys to our Toyota Sienna van, and ran out the door, leaving the girls fast asleep.

I vaguely knew the route he cycled home from Warner Brothers in Burbank where he had been putting in long hours completing the film *Maverick* with Mel Gibson. I pointed the car in the direction of Calabasas and drove. As I did so, I chastised myself for forgetting my shoes. The wood scorpions we'd seen in the back yard at the weekend flashed through my mind. Then there were the rattlesnakes.

More importantly, I thought, how was I ever going to find him without shoes? "That was stupid," I said out loud while continuing to accelerate. He'd tried to pronounce Calabasas correctly but was unable to say the name despite our having lived in LA for over a decade. How strange, I thought. Why had he muddled his words? He didn't sound drunk. What if he's in a ditch somewhere, and I can't find him? My mind raced in sync with the car's engine.

Just outside Calabasas, I pulled over along the only straight stretch of Old Topanga Canyon Road where it was safe to do so and turned off the ignition. If I didn't know where I was going, I argued with myself, how in the hell was I supposed to find him? Jumping out of the car, I realised it was darker than I thought it would be because this stretch of rural road didn't have any street lights. Turning the headlights on again, I scanned the road in front of me; not another soul in sight.

I paused for a moment and tried to listen for clues. All I could hear was a pack of coyotes wailing from somewhere far off to my right. Listening to their faint, high-pitched "woo, woo, woos" reminded me of Alaska. This helped give me strength and calmed my nerves, so I was able to think more clearly. Then, I noticed what looked like a dark patch of something wet near the middle of the road. Having driven it thousands of times before, it looked strange, so I decided to cross over to see what it was.

Still conducting heat from the day's summer sun, I felt the warm, gritty tarmac under my bare feet. I ran my hand through the pool of dark liquid: it felt wet and silky and darkened my palm. I raised it to my face to smell—fresh blood—and as I walked back to the car, I could just make out its crimson colour in the headlights.

"Charlie!" I cried out, breathlessly.

I followed the blood trail that led to the roadside opposite to where I'd parked the van. A rustling sound to my right sent me down the bank about ten metres, where I found Charlie and his bicycle crumpled up in a heap.

He was totally disoriented and speech-impaired when I reached him. I was so relieved to find him that it wasn't until I got both of us back to the van that I noticed blood was pouring from behind his left ear, and that the left side of his cycling jersey was soaked in it.

Less than ten minutes later, we arrived at the emergency room of Woodland Hills Medical Center. Charlie was taken in immediately and an x-ray confirmed that he'd fractured his skull. Badly concussed, he was put to sleep to rest his bruised brain, and he remained in critical care for the next forty-eight hours. The doctors told me that they needed to ensure that the bleeding on his brain and the swelling had stopped before he could be released.

I went home to relieve our neighbour, Cheri, from her hastily-acquired middle-of-the-night childcare duties. On the way, I stopped once again at the stretch of road where I'd found Charlie the night before. The heat of the morning sun was intense as I got out of the car; it was going to be another punishing August day. The now-dried pool of Charlie's blood on the road was more visible. Dazed, exhausted and angry, I stood in the road until the roar of a truck careening towards me shook me out of my stupor.

I then photographed the scene in case the images would be useful later, and also because I was unclear as to what had happened. Did he lose concentration from exhaustion or did someone hit him? I was hoping to understand what took place by returning to the site. Instead, all I could hear were the ER doctor's stinging words zipping around my brain.

"Charlie is lucky to be alive," he said. "A skull fracture of this magnitude is very serious. Next time, I hope he wears a helmet."

A kind of deep fury bubbled up in my chest as he said this. It brought back years of resentment of Charlie's stubborn refusal to wear protective gear when he cycled. The number of times I'd failed to persuade him to wear a helmet seemed pathetic at that moment.

"Don't do it for me," I repeatedly pushed him. "Wear it for the girls, at least!"

I'd bought him at least a half-dozen makes and shapes over the years in an attempt to find a helmet that was comfortable and acceptable to him. But, sporting their original tags, they just sat on the shelf of our bedroom closet.

There was also the concerned phone call from a friend a few months prior, telling me she'd seen Charlie without a helmet flying down Topanga Canyon Road on his bike.

"He must have been going at least forty kilometres an hour, Molly," she pressed. "Don't you know how dangerous that is?"

"Yes, I do," I responded, dryly. "Why don't you tell him yourself?"

Nothing anyone did or said seemed to make any difference, and he cycled unprotected daily. The helmet issue continued to be a source of fear and irritation for me as the years went on, but nothing I said or did seemed to matter. Even after his stint in the hospital, Charlie was determined to cycle his own way with the wind in his hair.

## Our September 11th

When Dr. Kline, supported by our midwife, Nancy, lovingly delivered Emma Louise and Francesca Alice on 3 August 2001 at Cedar-Sinai Medical Center in Los Angeles, we were overjoyed and grateful they were both healthy and strong, coming into the world peacefully.

Weighing 6.4 and 7.6 pounds respectively, Emma and Francesca rocked our world beyond anything we could have imagined. Overnight, we went from a family of four to absolute survival mode as we fed and cared for the twins around the clock while attempting to keep Isabella and Chiara's lives as normal as possible.

Fortunately, Charlie's mom and dad arrived from England to lend us a hand for the first two months. Just as they'd been for Charlie growing up, his parents were structured and meticulous about domestic duties and child raising, which proved to be a source of great comfort for us at the time. During those early weeks, after my breastfeeding at nine o'clock each evening, his mom would take the twins so I could sleep for a few hours, before bringing them back to me for another feed at midnight. This was a huge help as I tried desperately to synchronise their nursing schedules.

A few days before Charlie's parents were to return home, the events of 9-11 delayed their travel plans. As we watched the Twin Towers burn on the evening news, I was raw and exhausted. Earlier that day, we'd been rocked by a 6.4 magnitude earthquake, the largest one LA had experienced since 1994, which sent dishes and glassware flying off the tables, and books, vases and framed photographs off the shelves. Despite only minor damage, we'd spent most of that day carefully cleaning every corner of the house to make sure that the girls wouldn't hurt themselves on broken glass.

In spite of everything that was going on, or maybe because of it, I noticed that Charlie's mood swings had become more extreme. Sitting on the sofa next to him that evening, I felt that our world, too, was collapsing in around us.

## Blaming Charlie

After his parents returned to Europe, Charlie went into the spare bedroom, where he'd slept since before the twins were born, and stayed there for thirty-six hours straight, refusing my offers of food and water. I tried talking to him through the locked door, but he just mumbled something about how "it was all his fault."

"What's your fault?" I asked. "Come on, Charlie, answer me! Nothing is your fault," I tried to reassure him. Then I remembered the argument I'd had with his mother when she'd called Isabella "stupid" for pushing Chiara into the swimming pool. Maybe that's what he was upset about, I thought.

Charlie didn't answer me, so I returned to the kitchen where I'd been making dinner for the girls. They were quarrelling over who was going to hold which twin, and I knew they were getting hungry and tired.

When his TV director friend, Mark Jean, telephoned the next afternoon, Charlie emerged from the room to take the call. In the early days, that was all it took: a phone call from a director announcing that he wanted Charlie to edit his upcoming film. I'd watch Charlie's darkness melt away even before he finished the call, and a kind of determination would quicken his step for days afterwards. He had new energy that hadn't existed before.

These transformational calls forced me to question everything I knew about what was going on for him. If Charlie could switch it off that easily, didn't that mean he had control over his so-called depression? Didn't this mean he wasn't depressed after all?

Maybe he just hated his life, or maybe depression was just different from other diseases, such as heart disease, diabetes, or liver ailments, which we can't consciously switch off. Maybe it wasn't a disease at all. It certainly didn't behave like other physical illnesses.

More darkly, I sometimes wondered if nothing worked because it really was his fault. He had told me this often enough, and maybe I was starting to believe it. Even though I knew this was just the self-blame side of his depression talking, the thought crept into my mind every time frustration, fatigue, and pure "fed-up-ness" overtook me.

## A Stranger Arrives

The dark figure slid into the house wearing baggy clothes and dragging shadowy talons behind him. He took a seat on the sofa and stayed there. For a long time, I didn't know who he was. I could feel his blackness, but I couldn't see him clearly. I started to think that maybe Mom's prognosis of Charlie had merit. I never shared our struggle with her. I didn't tell anyone because I was confused by his appearance in our lives, and also because he soon seemed "normal."

Charlie's depression was like a Stranger. I was never sure how long he would stay and, each time, I was hopeful he'd only be there for a day or maybe two at the most. Yet, gradually, he began to stay for longer periods of time until, finally, he never left.

In the beginning, the Stranger was harmless enough. He was only around for a few hours at a time because something would happen–usually a phone call–and then he would swiftly leave. I can still feel the relief as I sensed him packing. Charlie would stand a little more erect, hold his head up higher, smile and even make a few jokes. That's how I knew the Stranger was almost gone.

Afterwards, I swiftly forgot he'd ever been there. For

a while, Charlie would be Charlie again. I would go back to doing what I'd always done, only with a lighter heart. Each time the Stranger disappeared, I was convinced he wouldn't return and there really wasn't a problem after all. I'd stop thinking about talking to someone or trying to find answers. In fact, I couldn't even remember the questions I'd had, and this would often carry on for weeks.

The next time the Stranger came to the door, however, he wasn't a stranger any more. I recognised him by his cower and the slinky way he slid into the house and planted himself either on the sofa or in the spare bedroom. I recognised the black suitcase he carried, which was much too heavy for his crumpled, light frame. The case he arrived with seemed bigger and heavier with each visit until, eventually, he was unable to stand upright at all. Hunched over, refusing to make eye contact, the Stranger's dark sneakiness made me think he had something to hide.

At some point, the Stranger moved into the spare bedroom permanently. When he did occasionally come out of the room, he wouldn't eat very much but always drank coffee. One morning, as I was making breakfast for the girls, the Stranger came into the kitchen and started preparing his morning brew. I knew immediately by the way Charlie moved that the Stranger had made an appearance during the night. Charlie's heaviness was all-pervasive and was only lightened slightly by an occasional deep sigh. He was trying to bring himself back into balance, I thought.

"Good morning, honey," I said, kissing him on the forehead. "Did you sleep okay?"

"Mmm, yeah, I guess."

Even though I could tell he hadn't slept, I didn't say so. I chatted about the day ahead, the weather, what the girls needed that day, and other random things. Aside from a few grunts, he didn't say much because he was too busy making one failed cappuccino after another.

One, two, three, four, five cups of subpar cappuccinos splashed across the bottom of our farmhouse sink that morning. I watched the dark brown, foamy liquids make interesting patterns against the white porcelain. It was one of those days, I thought: a Five Failed Cappuccino Day.

Once I realised what we were dealing with, I turned my attention to getting the girls sorted, readying myself for work and trying not to obsess about the Stranger's abrupt nocturnal arrival.

During the early years, I associated the Stranger's visits with actual life events. When Charlie was unemployed, the Stranger showed up more often and stayed longer. He also failed more cappuccinos. When Charlie loved the film he was working on or was planning a cycle ride or trip back to Europe, for example, the Stranger was nowhere to be seen. In this way, I convinced myself that Charlie was sensitive and prone to moodiness—and that was all there was to it. It just happened to him when things didn't go as he wished.

I also began to notice that the Stranger had a different communication style. Charlie was often talkative and lively, particularly at social events and with people he liked. He was especially chatty when his good friend Michael came over. When he was making coffee for Michael, even if it was a bad cappuccino day, he would chat the whole way through it. I could tell the Stranger had arrived, but I'm not sure Michael ever did because Charlie was his usual self during those times.

The Stranger often said things like, "What's the point?" or "It never works out for me." He was particularly fond of overusing the words "should," "always," and "never." I noticed that the Stranger was a master at downplaying accomplishments and good fortune. It was as if they'd never happened or that they'd somehow been vaporised. He was also an expert at dramatising setbacks and accentuating things we didn't want to happen. When I first became aware that the Stranger was doing this, I would try to reason with him to show how he was wrong and missing vital information. Annoyingly, I'd point out all the great things that had happened just a day, week or month ago, but he was adamant that I'd misinterpreted events. It never worked and, instead, I usually ended up questioning my own memories.

The Stranger was fixed in his views or, more accurately, couldn't see any other interpretation of events other than his own, and of these he was certain. This amazed me because sometimes I would hear Charlie tell me how excited he was to receive a call from one of such and such a director's top producers offering him a job. Then, if the Stranger showed up, within a very short time—sometimes even within a few hours—the description would sound something more like, "Oh, well, I wasn't that chuffed because it probably won't happen."

In this way, the Stranger began to take over our lives

and became more like an unwanted and highly destructive relative. We began to forget that he was just a visitor overstaying his welcome. The Stranger became way too familiar.

"Hadn't he always been there?" I sometimes wondered when he'd been in the spare room for over a week. Wasn't he part of the furniture, the walls, and foundation of our home? At those times, I'd try to remind myself that he was just a relative who needed to go home! We hadn't invited him in; he'd snuck in through the back door.

Over time, the Stranger began offering unsolicited advice–much as an unhelpful mother-in-law might. Charlie became hard-edged and defensive when the Stranger was around, questioning events rather than accepting them. When the girls quarrelled and it came to blows, for example, the Stranger interpreted this as unacceptable and spoiled. Charlie would have brushed it off as a spat between siblings. At these times, he criticised how I was parenting the girls and would tell me they needed more structure and earlier bedtimes.

On several occasions, I tried to talk to Charlie about how destructive it was to have the Stranger around. He nodded as I said so, but I knew he didn't know how to ask him to leave. And I couldn't do it for him. It was in this way that the Stranger moved in permanently.

## Half-Dead

Charlie started living as if he were only half-alive. In

looking back, I thought this must have been because he didn't want to be married to me and was unhappy.

I now realise that for much of his life, particularly when the Stranger was there, he only partially lived. He held himself back from nearly everything. Aside from cycling, coffee and films, he found little interest in anything else. Even though we could afford them, holidays and eating out were always "too expensive," he'd say. Playing games or going to the beach was "too tedious," and visiting friends or talking on the phone to family, "took too much time." He rejected most things.

Saying no to something can often open new doors and mean that we're more alive than ever. But for Charlie, the real way he said no to life was to stop making choices at all.

It happened subtly and over time, but now I realise that I would make the decisions for our family, and he would half-commit to them. This took place when we married, had children, bought a new car, renovated the house, built a pond, and moved to New Zealand, for example.

During conversations, I talked, and he nodded—or at least I thought he did. The story I told myself about his lack of contribution was that he processed decisions slowly and needed to think about them longer than I did. We'd put the issue or decision on hold, but we'd never revisit it. I would carry on as if a decision had been made. This is how we did everything and, mostly, it didn't occur to me that there was a better way to do things.

His half-commitments became a way a life for us both. It

wasn't until Chiara was born that I understood how flawed our decision-making process was and tried to pull back. Even though I enjoyed making decisions, I grew tired of carrying all the responsibility for them; I became weary of his disapproval of the outcome of decisions to which he hadn't contributed.

So, I embarked on an experiment. I convinced myself that he would step up and become more engaged with our family if I didn't do it for him. Instead of understanding Charlie's depression for what it was, I berated myself for being too strong and overriding him too often. For the first year after Chiara arrived, I stopped making major decisions. I quit working in order to let him earn the money to support the family, and I turned my attention to being a full-time mom. The extent of my decision-making revolved around what to cook for dinner each night.

After about six months of this, I gave up. To say that my experiment was an utter failure is an understatement. Instead of becoming more engaged and empowered, he became less so. His depression worsened, and he started to sleep most of the time. He stopped leaving the house altogether, and his job ended. I couldn't take it any more, so I abandoned my cause. The relief was incredible. I didn't know that the reason it hadn't worked was because it wasn't my fault in the first place. But it didn't occur to me at the time. I went back to doing things the way I'd always done them; it was a lot less frustrating that way.

I now see that as the Stranger became more entrenched,

the only thing he fully committed to was his own death. In this way, he made the most important decision of all.

Even though we're unaware of it at the time, in every moment of every day we make decisions to live or die. All the decisions we make, big or small, beyond what we eat, or whether or not to exercise, contribute to how alive we are each day.

We tend to think of life or death as absolute states of being but, in reality, we are somewhere on a continuum between them. We have both death and aliveness in us in varying measures at varying times. The thoughts we have, the beliefs to which we cling, the experiences upon which we fixate, and the meanings we make of those experiences, in particular, dictate how alive or dead we truly are. Understanding that living is a choice can help us avoid partial decisions and half-choices that lead to half-lived lives.

Understanding that we have a choice to die can crystallise our will to live. It can help us embrace our lives and live them as fully as we can while we are here. It can help us say no to living half-lives, or to half-living the lives we've been given, regardless of how long they may be.

Sometimes we choose to live half-dead. We hold ourselves back from people and experiences because we think they won't approve of us, or we justify that they're too risky or cost too much. We don't realise that in saying no to what we want, we're actually saying no to life itself.

## A Desperate Search for Answers

The year after the twins were born my mission was to find help. I worked to find something to even Charlie out, keep the Stranger at bay, and allow Charlie to more fully engage with our family. It wasn't until this point that I knew something deeper and more profound than just your everyday moodiness was going on for him, and yet I didn't understand it and was embarrassed to talk about it to anyone.

When the twins were almost a year old (after we'd moved to Topanga Canyon to free ourselves from the crippling mortgage of our Sherman Oaks' house), I did what I had always done when I was troubled by something; I read everything I could get my hands on.

I have always been a seeker. I love to read, think and explore the big questions in life. Why are we here? What happens when we die? This is a side of me that my father always encouraged. It's also helped me find a semblance of balance and certainty during a crisis and provides an outlet for the "doer" in me. But most of all, it gives me hope. I will be forever grateful to Dad for this.

There had to be an answer out there, I remember thinking, if only I could find it. I pored over every research paper. I reviewed the results of countless clinical trials on selective serotonin reuptake inhibitors (SSRIs), short for the antidepressant class of drugs. I knew that Zoloft, Paxil, Prozac, Celexa, Luvox, Lexapro and all the rest took at least three to four weeks to kick in. I spoke to psychologists, psychiatrists and practitioners from various therapies, including traditional psychology, cognitive behavioural therapy (CBT), acupuncture, and applied kinesiology, to name but a few.

Charlie was accommodating to my quest, yet half-hearted at the same time, which I put down to his being too down to help himself out of it. This was how I became in charge of his depression, as in every other area of our lives, and it only disempowered him more.

We hardly spoke about his depression directly which, in hindsight, sounds strange, yet it felt relatively normal at the time to just ignore it. Reluctantly, Charlie gave each antidepressant a go for at least six weeks at a time. He also agreed to take a high-dose regime of St. John's Wort, omega-3s, and s-adenosylmethionine (SAMe) to support his moods, remedies that had shown promise in clinical trials.

For six weeks at a time in 2002, we systematically and diligently went through each antidepressant that Charlie was prescribed. Each time he embarked on a new and promising tablet, we went into the "waiting for it to kick in" phase, then the "is it working yet?" phase, and finally reached the "sadly, no, it isn't working" conclusion.

It wasn't that the side effects bothered him, it was that they didn't change anything. "I still feel depressed," he would say, "but I just don't care as much."

For over a year, with the help of Dr. Best, a psychiatrist based in Woodland Hills, Charlie underwent a traditional form of psychoanalysis. At the same time, he spent months reading books such as *Toxic Parents: Overcoming Their*

*Hurtful Legacy,* and other books about family dynamics and their link to mental illness.

This dive into his past to understand his depression only made things worse. He gave me very few clues as to how he was getting on. I understood this was his private business; he never seemed to want to talk about it.

I noticed that each session only brought the Stranger in closer, extending his visits, heightening Charlie's negative self-talk and increasing his self-blame. A tangible, aching pain seemed to ooze from him and faults and fears were amplified. Pleasure and all semblance of happiness receded into the shadows. His mind's terroir became infertile, where nothing but negativity and dismay could grow.

## Trying Too Hard

I remember the day I made my mother laugh as if it were yesterday. It was rare for a number of reasons: firstly that she did so, secondly that I was the instigation of it, not one of her friends and, thirdly, because I hadn't meant to.

One afternoon when I was a teenager, Mom and I were in the kitchen scanning one of her favourite well-worn cookbooks, trying to decide which chocolate cake to bake. Flipping through the pages, I pointed to an old, dried blotch of brown that was streaked across a page from an earlier attempt, and said, "Oh, look, Mom, here's a sample we can try before we decide."

Mom burst into laughter, tilting her head to the ceiling

as she did so. It was a beautiful, unaffected laugh, and it caught me completely off guard. I continued to study her face long after the laugh left her lips and a smile had taken its place. As it did, a wave of long-lasting satisfaction and pride welled up inside me.

This light-hearted and brief moment we shared made a lasting impression on me because I realise now that there had been many failed moments before this when I'd tried to make Mom happy. It stopped me in my tracks because, aside from the times she drank martinis with her girlfriends, I couldn't remember a time Mom was light-hearted. It also struck me because I'd said it casually and in passing, without forethought or effort.

I've spent my life trying too hard at just about everything. There are some people who need to try harder, but I'm not one of them. I now see how forcing, pushing and working to be the best at everything was how my inner saboteur set me up for failure.

I used to compete with my little brother to see who could stack the books on our respective bedroom shelves the neatest. Mom had taught us to gradate the books from tallest to shortest. I added in colour coding and thickness criteria, too. My brother didn't care about any of it and, in this way, I always won my self-created contests.

There's nothing wrong with taking pride in what we do, but I now see how this obsession, which Charlie also shared, didn't allow me to enjoy success because there would always be better—someone or something. Another fundamental problem with having my inner perfectionist-turned-saboteur play the leading role in my life story was that, unlike the book stacking competition with my brother, I usually chose to take on challenges that I couldn't win.

My quest to make my Mom—and then later, Charlie—happy was not my job to tackle. I could be the funniest, smartest, and most beloved daughter or wife in the world, and it wouldn't have changed a thing. I know because I tried, and it only depleted me with feelings of inadequacy and failure.

## Sheer Frustration

The more we journeyed into Charlie's depression, the more dismayed I became with how little we understood about what was going on, and what we could do about it. I was also uncomfortable with the fatalistic way the mental health professionals were approaching it.

Every time he came home from an appointment, Charlie was worse. The Stranger's voice of self-blame grew louder and more adamant and, as Charlie had done many times before, he would withdraw from the girls and me.

One evening after a rather frantic meal preparation and a long day of work, I said something to him I will always regret. As part of a bigger conversation we were having about his general unhappiness, he referred to the psychologist he'd seen that morning as a "real tosser" and, he said, "You're not much better, Molly."

"If you're so unhappy here with us, why don't you just leave?" I screamed. "Piss off and leave the girls and me alone!"

I regretted those words the instant I said them, but it wasn't until Chiara's frightened five-year-old face popped up from behind the open refrigerator door that my self-condemnation set in.

## I Give Up

We continued to try different therapies to help Charlie, only to come out at the end of each one no better off, and a whole lot lighter in the wallet. After three years of this, I was done. Charlie refused to take any more drugs, and I stopped trying to make him do so.

I was exhausted from convincing him to try new things and from becoming angry when he wasn't as optimistic about his recovery as I was. "Why can't you just be happy?" I remember asking futilely one afternoon. To Charlie, this question was akin to asking him why he was born. It only fanned the flames of failure he carried everywhere.

Then there was the time in late August at our house in Topanga Canyon when the temperature hovered close to 43° C, despite the late hour. The Stranger was in the house and, after a night of pacing, Charlie had slept most of the day.

It was dinner time and our ten-month-old twins were hot, tired, hungry and extremely irritable. Despite my prodding, Charlie wouldn't tear himself away from his laptop screen.

There was a selfishness, or, more accurately, a self-centredness in Charlie that I couldn't stand when the Stranger was around. As I frantically flailed around trying to soothe two crying babies, I let out a yell that nearly shattered the hallway mirror, "Come on, Charlie! Grow some balls! Snap out it!"

There wasn't a whisper of sound anywhere in the house. We were silent, all of us, holding our breaths. Isabella and Chiara, who had up until that point been playing hide and seek in the living room, froze in their tracks as if they were playing a game of Freeze Tag. The twins stopped crying at the same time, and the crickets seemed to choke back their song in the night air. Those few moments drove my words deep into us all.

My heart sinks as I write this. I knew my words were unfair before they left my mouth. Despite the front he put on for others, it was a façade. Inside, Charlie was hurting, and my frantic outbursts were salt in a wound.

Not long after that incident, my medically intuitive sister, Sadie, told me she was concerned about me. She was right, and I knew it was time to shift gears. I was tired of waiting for Hollywood to ring and offer Charlie a job to usher in another "good patch."

## I Give in to Darkness

I was diagnosed with postnatal depression after Chiara

was born, and my doctor recommended medication. I strongly resisted and, at the same time, Charlie's experience had challenged my belief in the cure-all of herbs and natural medicine. But there was no way I was going to put drugs into my body, especially while breastfeeding; Chiara was only four months old at the time. So, I stumbled along through the dark, despite my daily concoction of natural remedies and a nutrient-dense, raw food diet that hadn't worked for Charlie.

But after the twins were born, it was worse. Everything was more exaggerated with two, especially my postpartum blues. After each restless night, I would sort out the girls and then return to bed to bury my head under the darkness of the pillow again. I struggled with nothing to look forward to. The insomnia was terrible. I was really not much good to anyone. I forced myself through the motions of living until, two to four months after the twins were born, I succumbed to the Stranger also.

Gradually and relentlessly, his darkness had crept into my every interaction with my friends and family. I knew happiness was out there somewhere but, just like Charlie, I couldn't find it. I saw no reason to get up in the morning, despite having four children under the age of five, and a husband who was so checked out from the latest antidepressant medication that he didn't notice.

When Emma and Checca, as we affectionately called her, slept, I was awake. I forgot what joy felt like and found myself looking past Emma's first smile. If my good friend, Delisa, hadn't pointed it out to me, I probably wouldn't have noticed. "Your family needs you, Molly," she urged. "You have to do something."

Thankfully, I'd hired a nanny when the twins were born; Maria was a godsend. If it hadn't been for the reprieve she gave me from the relentless childcare, domestic duties, and freelance consulting work, I probably would have been driven into the ground for good. You could have dug a hole and thrown the last handful of dirt over my dead body, and I wouldn't have cared.

Reluctantly, even though I was still breastfeeding the twins, when my doctor urged me to consider medication this time, my righteousness was too exhausted to protest. I began to take Sarafem, which is Prozac for new mums. It was only for postpartum depression, I rationalised to myself, not real depression. As an overachiever, an in-charge-of-my-life kind of person, I didn't do depression. That was Charlie's job.

I don't know when I had succumbed to the pressure of perfection, but my definition of it didn't have room for Prozac. Every day as I grabbed a Sarafem tablet, I reminded myself that this was just a moment in time. After all, I'd had four babies in six years, and I was run-down.

The meds were a way to keep going because the truth was that I didn't really trust Charlie to look after our family. Honestly, when the Stranger was in residence, I didn't trust Charlie to do much of anything. I half expected him to sell our assets to the next person who showed up at our front door. I had as much faith in him as he had in himself.

Unconsciously, I blamed Charlie for his inability to cope with life's ups and downs. And then, his failure became my own. For the first few weeks after starting antidepressants, I felt worse. I told myself that nothing I did mattered, and this was a humbling experience.

Despite Charlie's personal experience with them, however, mine was different. Once I could recognise myself again, my daily antidepressant ritual became easier and, besides, I told myself, it would only be until the postpartum period was behind me–maybe a year at the most

*"Emancipate yourself from mental slavery; none but ourselves can free our minds."*

- Bob Marley

## The True Self

There is what the child in us wants, which is different from what our adult selves want. Then there's what the true self wants: expansion and growth. Unlike our other selves, our true self is not our creation. According to author Sue Monk Kidd, it originates from something vast and benevolent that's beyond us. Our true self is our capacity for divinity and transcendence, constantly guiding us towards a wellspring of love and joy, knowing innately what we need at each step of the way. This universal life force is waiting for us to tune in and connect with it.

But if this benevolence is waiting for us, why is it so hard to live by the promptings of our true selves, as Herman Hesse pointed out? Sometimes there's a dilemma between who we think we should be and who we actually are. There is a struggle between our light and our shadow. In darkness, we believe we must squeeze our incredible magnificence into a peer group, a partnership, a family, or even a job. These "boxes" cannot reflect the light because they are too small and restrictive. Yet it's understandable that we try because this is what we see people doing all around us.

What we don't learn is how to embrace our uniqueness and love ourselves unconditionally in the fantastic form in which we arrived. I certainly didn't have this modelled for me. Instead, I absorbed the self-destructive thought patterns of the people I loved. Trying their best, they were unable to recognise the self-harm they perpetrated and the inner darkness they tried to escape.

Once we are able to hear our true selves, then we must bravely commit, marching forth hand-in-hand. And yet, it's difficult to step away from negative internalised programming because, at some point, we become perpetrators, too. Unless we choose differently.

And it is a choice. Do we remain imprisoned by our early programming, writing the same story with the same characters over and over again, or do we wake up and look at ourselves and the world around us in new ways? Do we choose to embrace the true self and allow it to carve our inner characters in a gentle and committed way, or do we ignore it altogether?

Having seen many people choose very different paths, I

know which one leads to suffering and darkness and which one to hope and healing.

## Seeds of Self-Doubt

I believe with everything I am that we are born perfect and stay this way, regardless of the stories we tell. Few would disagree that we start out this way, anyhow. If you really look at a baby, it's obvious. Despite the kind of birth she's had, the colour of her skin or physical features, each newborn oozes yumminess and perfection. Babies arrive hard-wired for love and growth without ever having to think about it. They are pure awareness and light.

Children don't wake up one morning and say, "Gee, I think I'll be loving today." It just happens. If you really stop for a moment and think about this, it's incredible. They know how to be, to love, to grow, and, as they do, they smile, walk, run, and play. Young children are completely authentic. They don't worry about what others think of them or wonder whether they're good enough. Babies don't try to be amazing; they just are. There is a purity and simplicity to an infant's essence that never truly goes away.

This perfection stays with us always, even if it becomes buried under mountains of self-judgements or the stories we tell. At some point early on, we begin to believe that we're only good enough if we behave in the ways the people around us expect. We buy into these messages from our teachers, friends, media and society. We begin to wear masks and play roles to be acceptable, and then we judge ourselves for doing so. We begin to carve off the pieces of ourselves that we don't like, stuffing them into our shadow or inner darkness. And even though we've forgotten what we've done, the seeds of self-doubt grow along the neural pathways of our fertile young minds which, up until that point, were open and receptive. We start trying to be what others expect us to be. We start telling ourselves lies, and this never feels good. Knowing that something is wrong, we begin to judge ourselves, often harshly.

Then our inner darkness spreads and seeps into our everyday interactions. And although we know it doesn't feel right, we don't even know it's happening. This is how the parts we can't see—the parts that lack the light—begin to take over our conscious minds, and we get lost in them, abandoning our true selves along the way.

If we do this long enough, we can launch into a journey of depression. If we practice guilt, shame, and self-criticism in particular, self-blame's neural pathways of negativity deepen and entrench upon our brains. They carve pathways that become well-worn with travel, leading to unpleasant places and experiences. They become dirt paths into forests of melancholy.

I saw this happen to Charlie. I witnessed first-hand how whatever we believe about ourselves becomes—in the end—our stories, our truth, our reality. Charlie's sense of personal failure was only his shadow that had hardened over time and sucked the life out of him. It was only a Stranger who had moved in and taken over his house.

# CHAPTER 4

# New Home, New Hope, New Zealand

*"Each day, we wake slightly altered, and the person
we were yesterday is dead."*

- John Updike

## Goodbye, America

In 2007, we started the process of moving halfway around
the world–far from the stress and strain of LA. In the
words of my extremely level-headed and loving sister-in-
law, Sian, "When something doesn't work, try something
new."

Before leaving, we farewelled our worldly belongings
from the Long Beach port for their six-week trip across
the Pacific Ocean to New Zealand. After parking the car,

a receptionist directed us to the far end of the container terminal where rows of massive cranes were lined up beside mountains of multi-coloured shipping containers stacked four and five high. My heart sank as I took in the scene, understanding that the enormity of the operation reflected the decision we were making, too.

Strangely, even though it was mid-summer, I felt a light mist of rain on my face. After rushing to get to the dock for our allocated loading time, the sprinkles felt cool and refreshing on my hot cheeks. I took the July rain as a sign that we were moving on to something unique, a better life. But I knew there was no certainty of it.

I watched the men in full-coverage overalls, high-vis vests, and hard hats remove our tables, chairs, pots and pans, couches, beds, appliances, books, garden pots, bicycles, and boxes of the toys and clothes from the moving truck and relocate them to wooden pallets before forklifting them into our cavernous container.

Seeing everything we owned stacked in a 12 x 3 metre metal box gave the move a finality that it hadn't previously possessed. It was as if we were sending all semblance of our life, and the happiness it contained, to float 11,000 kilometres to the other side of the world. I just hoped it would expand itself en route and meet us there.

When it came time for one of the workers to drive on the Mini Cooper, packed to the roof with Charlie's cycling paraphernalia, coffee machine, stereo, and music library consisting of thousands of neatly stacked vinyl albums, the car lurched forwards and stalled midway up the ramp.

Out of the corner of my eye, I saw Charlie cringe and look away. He had wanted to drive the car on himself but was told it was against terminal regulations. Only official dock workers, properly trained and fitted out, could complete the task. A few seconds later, after rolling back several metres, the engine turned over again and the car began to limp slowly up the ramp before vanishing into the dark belly of the container. Seeing its silver back end stall and then disappear made my heart lurch, too; I felt just as heavy.

Charlie loved living in Topanga. What if he didn't feel that way about Wellington, our new home? There was no guarantee that he would. I knew the girls and I would be okay, but was I crazy to push for a move of this magnitude? He didn't do change very well. He had half-agreed to the move but, like everything else, he was half-hearted and lukewarm about it. My enthusiasm had made it possible for all of us. I just hoped I hadn't misplaced it.

As the last of our belongings disappeared, we turned to leave and, as we did, the sky darkened, releasing torrents of hard raindrops that felt more like hail. By the time we got back to the car, we were soaked to the skin. Sitting in the driver's seat, dripping, I reminded myself that we'd made the decision because I knew there must be some-where in the world that would make us happy–somewhere our darkness couldn't follow.

## A Stay-at-Home Dad

Our new house was outside Wellington, New Zealand's

capital city, in Ohariu Valley, on a three-acre block of land next to a deer farm. It was rural, unfamiliar, cold and windy. Unfortunately, none of these qualities inspired Charlie in the way that I'd hoped. I had convinced myself that New Zealand was the answer to our problems, and the last chance to keep our family intact by living in a saner way, far away from the stress of Hollywood.

Aside from his girls, Charlie had few great loves in his life: cycling, movies, music, and espresso. I'd always believed that if he maintained a decent quality and quantity of each, everything would always turn out right.

Charlie was passionate about film-making and music, but it was mostly through cycling that he self-medicated his depression when nothing else worked. Despite the unforgettable look of achievement on his face the day he made it to the top of Alpe d'Huez, the Tour de France's iconic mountain climb, I hadn't truly understood the profound healing power of those rides for him. For years, in fact, I resented his fifty-mile-a-day, four to five times a week rides, until the day came that LA's sunshine, and his dear friend and cycling buddy, Michael, were on the other side of the world.

Despite buying himself a set of $500 rollers for indoor cycling on his top-of-the-line Colnago racing bike, after our move to New Zealand, he gave it up in less than a month. I remember he said that he hated cycling in New Zealand because all he noticed were the huge electricity pylons that dominated the hills around our house. I hadn't even seen them, but after that, I would sometimes catch him staring silently at the poles visible from our kitchen window.

Like everything to do with his depression, it seemed to happen gradually, over time, and without much fanfare. When he gave up cycling, alarm bells should have gone off in me, but I was busy getting the girls settled into a new school and returning to work full-time.

We'd decided that in between editing jobs for Weta Workshop, a special effects company based in Miramar, Charlie would be a stay-at-home dad.

## Giving Things Away

One of Charlie's first tasks in his new role as a stay-at-home dad was to get us organised. I was working long hours and finding it difficult to wait for our container ship to arrive and be released from Wellington Harbour. Our belongings were still more than four weeks away.

In the meantime, we lived in a house where we couldn't find anything. The dishes were stacked in the bathroom, our clothes were piling out of suitcases and trunks, and we were sleeping on the floor in sleeping bags borrowed from my co-workers.

To make things easier, Charlie purchased office filing boxes from the local stationery store and began organising our clothes in them. One evening after work, I walked into the bedroom and found a red cardboard box with the words "The Queen's Knickers" written in black marker pen on the top and sides. There was even a simple drawing of a crown next to a pair of underpants. The girls had theirs, too. He'd made each daughter a different coloured box with her own illustrations neatly drawn beside the words: Princess Isabella's, Chiara's, Emma's, and Checca's Knickers.

As I looked at my box, I smiled, knowing that it was a reference to one of our favourite books, *The Queen's Knickers,* by Nicholas Allen. We had read it to the girls so many times that Charlie and I could recite it off by heart. It tells the story of a Queen who likes to dress smartly and owns an enormous dresser of drawers for keeping her vast knicker collection in. She also employs a helper to look after her knickers full-time.

Every morning for many months as I reached into my cardboard underwear box, I reassured myself that Charlie was improving and that our family was becoming happier, too. The move had been the right thing to do.

Shortly after I became aware of my daily ritual, however, Charlie took a turn for the worse. After initially embracing his new role, he began to give things away. One evening after a long day, I came home to find that he was re-homing his three bicycles, most of his cycling clothing, his tool chest and five of his six pairs of shoes. That night I prepared dinner for us while he repeatedly answered the doorbell to complete each transaction. I wasn't aware that he'd put his possessions on the online marketplace, Trade Me, several days earlier. At least four different purchasers arrived at the house that evening to pay for and haul away his belongings.

When I asked him why he was getting rid of them, especially his beloved bicycles and riding gear, he just stared at me blankly and muttered, "I don't need them any more."

A wave of sadness flooded through me with these words. I knew it was confirmation that I was wrong about the improvements we were making, but it wasn't until he stopped getting out of bed every morning and refused to take the girls to school that I started to panic.

## A Cry Out to Crisis Assessment

We'd been in our new home less than six months when I placed the call to the Ministry of Health's Crisis Assessment Team (CAT), seeking an urgent assessment for Charlie. The Stranger's now well-worn mantra about how the girls and I would be better off when Charlie was gone had turned paranoid.

I found him eavesdropping from the hallway closet one morning as I spoke to his brother, Bob, on the phone. This confused me, and so did the fact that he'd stopped eating altogether, only drank coffee, and looked as if he were imploding into himself. I wondered if the Stranger had somehow morphed his depression into some else entirely.

"Hi," I said quickly to the lady on the other end of the phone, to get past the pleasantries as fast as possible. "I need an urgent mental assessment for my husband. I think he's suicidal, and I'm really scared."

"Will he agree to come in and see us?" she asked.

"No, he won't," I strained.

When we'd moved to New Zealand, Charlie had told me that he wouldn't take any more antidepressants, see any more experts or do anything else, for that matter. "You can drag me to a million doctors, Molly. It won't work," he'd said, emphatically, only a week before. We were returning home from a doctor's appointment and a trip to the chemist to get another refill of his sleeping meds when he announced this.

Jerking the car over to the side of the road, I slammed on the brakes and yelled, "You have to keep trying. Not for me, not for you, but for the girls! You don't have a choice!" As my words echoed around inside our Fiat Multipla, I was shocked to hear how desperate and dictatorial I'd become.

The lady on the phone told me, "I'm sorry, then. There's nothing we can do."

"What do you mean, there's nothing you can do? Can't you come and do some sort of assessment on him like your name suggests?"

"No, because he would have to agree to come see us, or we would have to take him against his will from your house and that would be too upsetting for everyone in your family, including your children, wouldn't it?"

A shudder of panic punched me in the stomach as the image of Charlie being dragged out of the house flashed through my head.

"What can I do then?" I asked, breathlessly.

"I'm really sorry, but if you've already contacted your family doctor then there's nothing we can do."

"What? Do you mean I have to wait until he's hanging from a goddamn tree before you guys do something?!" I slammed down the phone without waiting for her reply.

The sofa I'd been sitting on suddenly felt suffocating. I pulled myself out of its deep cushions and began to pace the length of the large Turkish rug that Charlie's parents had given us when we married.

Was that it? I wondered in disbelief. Were there no other options? Was that really the extent of New Zealand's mental health services? Wasn't there *anyone* who could help us?

When someone has a heart attack the authorities send an ambulance straight away, right? Isn't that how things are supposed to work? Apparently not when someone is suicidal. But isn't the potential outcome exactly the same: death?

Maybe that just happens in the movies, I thought. Recently I'd certainly felt like I was seated in a dark room watching the deterioration of our New Zealand life flash before me on a large screen. As I continued to stare at the rug under my feet, one thing became crystal clear: we weren't in Hollywood any more.

## Lying to Ourselves

Winter was on its way. Despite the dapple of sunshine

breaking through heavy cloud, the air felt cold. Although only 4 p.m., it was nearly dark. The days had grown short, taking my patience with them.

Having no idea what to do, I sat on the edge of the bed and looked at him. I no longer recognised the thirty-kilo body on the 168 cm frame that sat next to me. Charlie's skin was translucent and pale, ashen grey. His once gorgeous green eyes were now dull, foggy and sunken as if they had shifted at least three centimetres closer to the back of his brain.

I glanced out of our bedroom window to see the bare branches of the kowhai tree fly about in the strong wind at the edge of our pond. The memory of the glorious, tubular-shaped yellow flowers that had filled its limbs last spring felt surreal. Had this barren cluster of sticks really produced such splendour as I remembered or, like everything else at the time, had I deceived myself? Were those blossoms just another way I'd tried to sugarcoat our move to New Zealand?

Our new life was beginning to crumble, just like the old one. The words worming out of Charlie's mouth didn't make sense.

"You'll be better off without me," he kept saying.

He then recited a long list of personal failures for which he could never forgive himself: the unplanned pregnancy that sent us to the family planning clinic; his poor marks at school that instigated the cruelty of his teachers (the "Brothers"); the Stanley Kubrick film he never worked on;

the Hollywood career that didn't meet his expectations; the move from London to Los Angeles to pursue his dream of becoming a film director; and even our recent move to New Zealand, the "end of the Earth," as he called it.

A great lesson for me is that we take ourselves with us wherever we go but, at the time, this harsh reality offered no comfort. As I continued to listen closely to his words, intense nausea seeped into my bones, spread to my stomach and crept into every cell of my body, so much so that I felt I could have thrown up for hours from the depth of my soul. When did everything become such a failure to him?

"You'll be better off when I'm gone, Molly," he repeated. "So will the girls."

With these words, soft tears welled up from the dark pools under his eyebrows. He loved Isabella, Chiara, Emma, and Francesca with all his heart. Despite the haze and confusion of his depression, of this I was sure.

The full force of denial kicked in at that moment. "What are you talking about?" I shouted, referencing the film his friend and director, Jonathan King, had asked him to edit up in Auckland, 640 kilometres north.

"You'll only be gone for a few months, and then you'll be back home. Besides, the break from us will do you good."

The look on his face said everything, and it was at that moment I knew we were in deep trouble. There was no going back.

## A Very Dark Day

It was unusually late as Charlie and I stood at the sink washing the dinner dishes. I hadn't arrived home from work until almost eight, and it was one of those days when Charlie hadn't functioned well.

The house was a disaster. The girls were feral, and there was nothing to eat. By the time I had cleared a pathway to the kitchen from the front door, torn Emma off the back of Francesca, and slapped together a few peanut butter and jelly sandwiches for dinner, I was absolutely stuffed.

The girls wolfed down their sandwiches and, thankfully, Isabella went upstairs to make sure they brushed their teeth.

Charlie reached for my arm and leaned into my chest. He felt especially drawn and thin as he whispered, "You'll be better off without me. I've had a very dark day, Molly," he muttered.

I pulled him closer into my body and tried to hold his small frame for a few moments. He was all bone, and I could only just feel his chest rise and fall and make out a faint heartbeat.

Even so, I couldn't face his dark day just then. In a half-hearted and rushed way, because I knew how much Wellington's wet and windy weather was getting to him, I responded with something like, "Yes, it's been gloomy, dark and rainy for a week, but tomorrow it'll be better."

I then turned away and said, "Honey, I really need to get the girls in bed now. Let's talk about it after I have them settled, okay?" Then I went upstairs.

I kept going, just like I always had.

## The Search

I'd meant to go back downstairs to Charlie, where he was watching TV. But after Emma and Checca had fallen asleep, I must have dozed off, too. It was after 2 a.m. when I left the twins' room and stumbled to our empty bed.

At 6:11 the next morning, I knew before I opened my eyes that something was different. A shiver of dread rushed through me as I thought about the previous night and the talk we'd never had. The vision of his strained and tautly-drawn face raced through my mind. I headed for the kitchen to make breakfast as per usual.

I heard the girls getting dressed for school upstairs as I cracked an egg in a glass bowl. Just like every other morning, they sounded more like a small herd of elephants than our offspring. I tried hard to put everything out of my head and pretend it was just another ordinary weekday morning at the Irelands'.

"Time for breakfast, guys! Come on!" I yelled impatiently up the stairs. "Scrambled eggs and toast."

More often than not, I felt like a drill sergeant barking orders. Lately, I'd been going through the motions in body only and really needed to talk to someone, I thought.

The girls splashed into the kitchen like water shaken off a wet dog. Maya, our large six-month-old border collie puppy, was jumping excitedly all over them. Her wagging tail narrowly missed the plate of toast I was placing on the table. She was a distraction for the girls and had only been with us for a few weeks. I need to remember not to acquire any more pets during stressful times, I told myself.

I glanced at the windowsill above the sink and there–lined neatly in a row–were Charlie's cell phone, car keys, wallet, and a sealed manila envelope. Instantly, my field of vision went dark. I hunched over the sink to catch my breath before running to the bedroom to call our friend, Tara. Within minutes, her silver Mitsubishi Pajero was idling in the driveway.

"Okay, guys, change of plans," I announced, as the girls waited for me to drive them to school. "Tara is going to take you today, instead."

Then, the second they were out of the house, I started to search.

*"In guilt, we say no to life."*

- Joan Borysenko

# Blaming Ourselves

We make up stories about the way we think things are, and

then blame ourselves when they don't go according to plan. If I could really be "The Boss of the Whole World" (as Isabella once referred to me) one of my first jobs would be to banish guilt as the most destructive force on Earth.

The most crippling side effect of suicide is the self-blame it leaves in its wake. The pebble that drops in the pond affects anyone and everyone who has ever known the person. Depending on the size of the splash, guilt travels fast and, as it does so, spreads shame far and wide with its ripples. The moment we hear about an individual taking his or her own life, we replay every interaction we've ever had with him or her; not only the experiences, but every word we exchanged, and every piece of information we ever knew.

We run the news of the loss past our personal reference points with them and replay our memories over and over again, depending on how close, or how far from the centre of the pebble drop we were. Regardless of the intensity with which we do this, the fact is that we do so tenaciously. Absolutely everyone who knew Charlie in any capacity, large or small, was impacted in this way. Those closest to him suffered from these incessant and damaging internal voices the most.

On learning about a loved one's suicide, a conversation with a close friend or relative sounds something like this:

"I wish I had been nicer to him the last time I saw him."

"I was so caught up in my own life that I didn't reach out to him when I should have."

"How could I have done this? He must have really

needed me."

"God, I'm selfish."

"Why didn't I just pick up the phone and call instead of sending that email?"

"I was going to visit New Zealand, LA, London, Timbuktu, etc., to see him. Now I really wish I had."

This is one way we make up stories. If my personal inter-actions with the person had been more supportive, closer, loving, patient, kind, whatever, then maybe I could have made a difference. Maybe he would still be here today.

The thinly-masked underbelly of this process is that somehow, in some way, I am to blame.

# Chapter 5

# Losing Charlie Forever

*"Just as ripples spread out when a single pebble is dropped into water, the actions of individuals can have far-reaching effects."*

- Dalai Lama

## We Wait

The next twenty-four hours will remain etched in my memory for eternity: the plea to our Kiwi friends, Jamie and Jonathan, to see if they knew where Charlie was; the call to 111, New Zealand's emergency services number; and most of all, I remember the wind.

The strong southerly that rolled into Wellington's Ohariu Valley early that morning howled my despair from the roof. Thankfully, Jamie and his wife, Melissa, had dropped everything to be with me as a team of policemen searched for Charlie.

Wellington's gales, which are especially strong with each change of season, only seemed to frazzle my already shot nerves. Wellington's "four seasons in one day" saying is accurate. When we first moved there, Charlie and I used to laugh as we recalled the struggle LA's TV weathermen had to come up with another way of saying the same thing: fine and sunny. New Zealand's weathermen have another challenge: how to describe different levels and types of wind.

I'd always hated strong wind. When I was a kid, I remember our good friend, Virginia, "Bunny," telling me during a fierce storm in Anchorage, that she'd made friends with it when she was growing up in Nome. Perched at the edge of the Bering Sea, Nome had taught Bunny to see the beauty and poetry in the wind, something that inspired me, yet seemed very far out of reach just then.

As the police searched for Charlie, each wind gust amplified my fear and accelerated the roller coaster of dread and dismay that swelled inside me.

The police were incredibly kind. While his officers went through our outbuildings and multiple paddocks, a senior sergeant sat with us at the kitchen table, going through all the possible options for Charlie's whereabouts.

"Maybe he's gone somewhere to clear his head," the sergeant suggested. Since everything but his gumboots,

Union Jack beanie hat, and mustard yellow Patagonia jacket were still at the house, the possibilities, according to the sergeant, were unlimited.

Listening to sergeant's empty words, I watched the macrocarpa trees at the back of our hill paddock violently sway in unison with each wind gust, just like a conductor's baton at the height of a symphony score's crescendo.

I hadn't opened the envelope, nor had I told the police that I'd found Charlie's wallet, keys and cell phone on the windowsill that morning. If I could erase them from my memory, maybe the necessity for the search would disappear as well.

Multiple cups of tea were poured as the hours dragged by, and we waited for news.

## Receiving the News

It was nearly dark and still no word. Tara had brought the girls home from school and was playing Monopoly with them in the adjacent lounge. Melissa was roasting a chicken in the kitchen. Jamie lit a fire to chase away the chill of the evening air, and our hopes of finding Charlie were fading. All I could do was sit in the dying light and stare at the embers reflecting against the curtains.

Suddenly, Melissa escorted the police sergeant into the den, where he pulled out the bench of my mother's upright Steinway piano and perched on its edge. I scanned his kind face intently and sucked in my breath.

"We've found Charlie," I remember him saying—before the room went dark.

## Venom

In the minutes that followed, the details of Charlie's demise emerged, then it became like putting together the pieces of an intricate puzzle. He must have left the house and climbed the hill behind our house at about 11 p.m., as I slept.

In an effort to ease my disbelief, I prompted the officer to tell me the whole, plain, awful truth in vivid detail. I don't remember exactly what he said, something to the effect that our neighbour had found him hanging half-way up an electricity pylon on her small Highland cattle ranch.

What I do remember is the venom and denial with which I responded. "How do I know you're not making it up?" I blurted, obnoxiously. "I want to see him. I don't believe you! I can't believe you!"

"I've got to make sure you're not lying!" I finally yelled, before starting to cry.

The sergeant's eyes were warm and full of compassion. His voice was soft. "You will, Mrs. Ireland," he said, calmly. "You will."

## Wellington Hospital Morgue

At some point on our way to Wellington hospital to

identify Charlie's body, I went numb. As I watched the city lights blur before me in a dark haze, my limbs began to tingle and then evaporate. As we drove through the rain, I felt like I was hovering several feet above Jamie's silver BMW.

Despite the horror of the situation, I needed to see Charlie. There was a piece of me that couldn't believe he was really gone until I'd looked at him with my own eyes.

Jamie pulled into the parking garage, and he and Melissa headed towards the long corridor to the wing in the basement where the city morgue was located. I was grateful that I could still operate my legs to follow.

And just like that, without fanfare, we met one of the morticians and were led into a large, open room with high ceilings, which was separated from smaller rooms by floor-to-ceiling windows, each with individual hospital beds. Most of the beds were empty, except for the one in the far corner, where Charlie's badly bruised body lay.

In a split second, I released Melissa's hand and lurched at the window separating his body from me. Slamming my fist hard against the glass, I let loose a primal sounding wail that I didn't recognise as my own. I then threw myself against the glass and started to sob. That pane kept me from his body and my dreams of ever being with him again.

I would replay the horrific vision of his black and blue neck and face with his tongue hanging out of his mouth over and over again in my mind for a long time.

"How could you? How could you hurt yourself so badly?!"
I screamed. "How could you do this to your beautiful body?
How could you do this to the girls? How could you do this
to us?"

On that Wednesday 28 May 2008 at about 6:30 p.m.,
time stood still. And the life I'd known for over eighteen
years ceased to exist.

## Telling the Girls

I don't remember much of what happened over the next
few days. I went through the motions of phoning Charlie's
parents. His brothers, Robert and John, were on their way
from London to New Zealand. Then I told the girls that
their Daddy wouldn't be coming home.

"Where is he?" six-year-old Francesca insisted, as I
struggled to stay composed.

"He's gone to Heaven," I said, trying to do so as mildly
as possible. "Daddy was very sick, and now he can rest
and find some peace at last."

"You mean because it's quiet up there?" she pressed.

"Something like that, honey," I said, not sure how to
respond.

"Is that why he was limping last week?" Emma piped up.

Not knowing what she was referring to, I responded,

"Yes, when people are ill, sometimes they struggle to keep going. They get tired."

"I'm glad he's having a long sleep, then," Emma said, sweetly. "That's important, right, Mommy?"

"Yes, it is important, honey, but I'm afraid Daddy isn't sleeping."

Up until that moment, the older girls, Isabella and Chiara, had just been staring at me blankly. When I glanced in their direction to see how they were doing, they began to sob in unison. With Emma on one knee, Francesca on the other, and one arm each around Isabella and Chiara, I pulled them so close to me that I thought I would break into four pieces. We clung to one another until I went numb, and I vowed never to let them go.

I kept telling myself over and over again, "Cry, my beating heart, but please don't break."

## A Haka

In the days that followed, I tried to figure out how to help us all say goodbye. My dilemma was that I knew without question that nobody would believe he had taken his own life. I struggled to believe it. He had become practiced at wearing his "I'm okay" mask and, together, we were good at hiding his depression, especially in our new home country. Nobody knew.

Despite everything I had gone through with him, if I had

not seen his mangled neck and empty, bruised shell with my own eyes, I wouldn't have believed it, either. How did I expect the girls to accept that he was gone? I had heard stories of tragic grief where the loved ones kept thinking the deceased would reappear one day. I didn't want this for the girls, Charlie's family, or myself, for that matter.

Three weeks earlier, Isabella, Chiara and I had been to a memorial service for an eighteen-year-old girl. She was a new acquaintance from their Pony Club and her seemingly impulsive suicide shocked us. It also challenged everything I knew about suicide because her journey was so sudden, without any apparent depression leading up to it. It couldn't have been more different from ours.

Her memorial service took place at a local high school, where she was about to graduate. Apart from the anguish of her parents and sister, the thing that struck me the most was the haka at the close of the ceremony. If you've experienced one in real life, or more accurately, felt New Zealand's traditional Maori war cry, the haka, you will never forget it. And this one was especially moving because behind it was all the anguish and despair of a community who had just lost a young person, senselessly, because she had hanged herself in a neighbour's barn.

I felt the roar of the wind on my cheeks as the high school "warriors" gathered to perform their haka challenge outside the school auditorium. The energy was electric as the chant of overwhelming grief flew out of their mouths. They shouted the war cry, sending sparks of energy down my spine and tears streaming down all our faces. With each slap to their thighs, punch to the air and lash of their tongues, they told a story more powerful than anything that could have been relayed by words alone.

Newland College and every inch of Wellington's northern suburbs shook with rage that day. Regardless of whether or not we opened our mouths, we all shouted:

"This is wrong at every level! How can life be so very cruel?"

## The Goodbye Envelope

When I finally had the courage to open the envelope, a wave of desperation flooded me. My body shook uncontrollably as I felt the smooth, cool surface of the paper in my hands. For much of that first day, or maybe longer, it just sat there next to his wallet and keys.

Earlier, I had found on the kitchen table the receipt from the hardware store where he had purchased ultra-high-molecular-weight polyethylene rope on the day he hanged himself. Looking at it carefully, the only way to describe the devastation I felt, and the sense of disbelief that washed over me, was as if a massive cyclone had finally hit land.

I could hardly bring myself to open the envelope, partly because I already knew what was in it, and partly because, then, it would be official; it really would be true. I would have to admit failure and look it square in the face, putting a stop to the wait for the phone calls that never came.

It wasn't sealed, so I slid the envelope's contents out

onto the table. There was a yellow sticky note that read: "What Molly Needs." Then a list of online banking passwords and his will, outlining his desire to be cremated, signed and dated two weeks earlier. That was all–just the things we would need to keep going and carry on without him.

Wait, I wondered, where was the goodbye letter? Hadn't he even written me a quick note to say he really did love me after all? What about a note to the girls that I could save for them until they were older? I know for sure he loved *them*.

Several weeks later, I found a letter on his laptop, dated 25 May 2008. He'd managed just one half-written, partial sentence:

*"My Dearest Molly: You know how you said this move was our last chance to save our family, well . . ."*

I felt both crazy and utterly devastated after reading this. The rejection and abandonment were intolerable. I felt like a pile of excrement that had been flushed down the toilet of eternity. I'd been discarded into the sewer of Hell, and I felt worthless and soiled. These words, or lack thereof, were definitive proof that he really didn't love me after all.

I had so many questions that only he could answer, yet he left me without any explanation. He left me without a goodbye; nice knowing you; thanks for having my babies; thanks for loving me for eighteen years. But there was nothing, not even a full sentence.

I believed I was too strong, too dominant, and took too much away from him: his independence, dignity, and self-respect. As a result of this story I told myself, I reined myself in so that he would step up to the plate, but he never did.

I must have been wrong about all of that. The only thing I knew for certain afterwards was that I didn't know a thing. My sense of failure was absolute.

For all those years, I'd lived a lie, a lie so huge that the hollowness of the hole it left in me has been excruciatingly difficult to fill. My story of being unlovable loomed large and dominated my entire life, even as I pretended differently for the girls.

"What is to give light must endure burning."

Viktor Frankl, MAN'S SEARCH FOR MEANING

## The Hard, Cold Truth

For as long as I could remember, I'd done things to please other people. I enjoyed making them happy, I told myself. The hard, cold truth was that I needed people to appreciate and validate me. I sought approval to feel good about myself.

With Charlie's death, the absolute worst had happened, and it freed me, in a way. It helped me put aside what everyone else wanted from me, how everyone else thought

I should talk about the situation and, instead, to say good-bye to him, as best I could, for the girls and me.

This was incredibly scary because I was told repeatedly "not to say so much," that it would be better this way. "You're too honest, Molly," one of my neighbours said to me while dropping off a care package for the girls one morning.

Then there was the phone call from his family in Europe, requesting that I not tell his extended family the truth of how he died. "Just say he had a car accident," I remembering hearing in disbelief, "or maybe something to do with his heart."

I was stunned.

Those words filled me with an intense sickness that seemed to be a violation of every fibre of my being. Underneath their desire to hide the truth, I imagined their unspoken accusations that somehow it was my fault and, somehow, I shouldn't have let this happen.

Perhaps for the first time in my life, I didn't care what people said. I did what I thought best. I brought home what was left of him.

## A Sacred Homecoming

I was upset when I was told that I couldn't have a haka at Charlie's funeral for a number of reasons; primarily, because you need to have met beforehand the people who perform it for you, and he was already gone. I did, however, adopt another traditional Maori funeral practice: an open casket.

For three days, his body graced the small room that housed my large collection of books at the back of our house. Sliding kauri wood doors allowed the room to open into the adjacent lounge.

The priest from St. Benedict's Catholic Church, our local parish, accompanied the tall, dark-suited men from the funeral home, and the girls and I gathered around with family and close friends. Candles were lit. Prayers were said. The funeral home had dressed his body in his favourite cycling jersey and Lycra shorts for the occasion. Charlie's bright yellow Colnago racing cap topped off the outfit.

The caretakers had done a good job of covering the severe bruising to his face and neck. He was even clean-shaven, which bothered the girls and me because we rarely saw Charlie without a heavy, dark stubble—he looked too squeaky clean.

Charlie's brothers, Robert "Bob's Your Uncle," and John John, arrived from London that evening, along with my dad and sister, Erica. I was so pleased to see them. I needed them there just as much as I needed my girls to see for themselves that Daddy was gone. I spent the next few days lighting candles and re-opening the sliding doors every time someone slid them shut. Everyone who visited us during this time was encouraged to "talk" to him or spend time saying goodbye.

As strange as it was from a Catholic perspective, bringing Charlie home was an amazing experience that I wouldn't change for anything. A steady stream of people, mostly from overseas, came with love and hugs for us, including our close friends, Michael and Gillian, and Jack and Michelle from Topanga. Those who couldn't come in person telephoned and sent poems, emails, and photographs containing memories of better times. The fortitude we managed at the time to make all this happen can only be put down to the incredible love and support we had from everyone around us. I know we were graced by a force much larger than ourselves, as well.

Uncle Bob strummed George Michael's "Faith", along with Charlie's other favourite songs, on the guitar. His music was a potent healing balm for us, and I know without a shadow of a doubt that it was delivered from the voices of our guardian angels. Surrounded by family and friends, the girls and I huddled together for hours on bean bags in front of a roaring fire, listening to Bob play. It filled our house with a sense of sacredness, and for the first time since we'd moved from Los Angeles, the place felt like home.

Without any prompting, Isabella and Chiara organised Emma and Francesca to place some of Daddy's favourite things in the coffin next to him. It was incredibly moving to watch their growing ease and confidence around him, following repeated trips to the kitchen to collect coffee beans, chocolate, and bottles of wine to place gently by his side. Auntie Sian helped them find pens, markers, and other art supplies, so they could write notes and draw pictures on his coffin lid. A bottle of Grolsch (his favourite beer) wedged tightly under his right armpit made me smile.

As part of his house husband duties, Charlie had started teaching film-making to students at the girls' school, St Benedict's, which was nestled in the hills overlooking Wellington's harbour. He was popular with the kids, and the teachers loved him, too. Because of this, a few families visited during that time, placing small gifts and artwork in his coffin. It made me grateful for the extended network of loving souls who congregated with us during that dark time.

Having Charlie at home catapulted our healing, creating a space to focus on the person he had been and the loss we shared. I am forever grateful for the family and friends who sat with the girls and me at that time and just cried with us. When we were all together, I felt safe and loved—something I hadn't felt in a very long time—and I soaked it up.

For three days, there was no dodging, no second-guessing, no turmoil, no denial. I literally stared my loss straight in the face and held it close. I talked openly about my memories and, through this time of loving acceptance, my pain faded into the background. I faced the reality of the situation directly and honestly, allowed the magic to unfold and all my anguish and fear to vanish... or so I thought.

Even though the weather had been sunny for the entire three days he was home, when it was time for Charlie to go—just minutes before the dark-suited men sealed off his coffin and carried it out the front door—the heavens unloaded their fury.

The wind howled with such force that Uncle John had to heave the front door ajar and hold it there to let them out. The rain bucketed down and then the hail started. Heavy, white pellets pounded the girls and I and the ground all around us as we followed his coffin to the hearse idling in the driveway. And for what seemed like forever, the sound of frozen ice drilling into the top of the car as it pulled out of the drive beat a raw sense of loss deep into my soul.

## The Funeral

In the mirror above my dresser I caught the reflection of our pohutukawa tree flailing about in the wind outside the window. It was fitting that Wellington's southerlies were especially strong that afternoon. They reflected my turmoil.

Aside from a few branches that had been stripped bare by possums, this New Zealand "Christmas tree" stood nearly fifteen metres high and was full of dark greenish-blue leaves with silvery-white underbellies. It had been thick with masses of bright red, brush-like flowers when we moved into the house the previous December.

My neighbour, an ardent gardener, Vivian, who was about halfway through a twenty-year process of returning her paddocks to native bush, told me that the pohutu-kawa was sacred and that this one was very old, possibly more than 100 years.

Looking at it now, I wondered how it had withstood for so long such beatings from the aggressive winds. As I watched it bend and bow under the turbulent lashings, I took a deep breath and thought about how I was going to get through the next few hours. How could I sit through a ceremony that would confirm once and for all that he was gone? How was I going to endure the stares of all those people who couldn't possibly understand how much I'd wanted to save him?

As I thought about Charlie's cremated remains, I wondered where his ashes would ultimately disperse like the thin, brown pohutukawa seeds that were flying about in the wind. Given his strict Catholic upbringing, I was surprised when I read in his will that he wanted to be cremated, but I figured he'd already lost all faith.

To the Catholic Church, suicide is a *moral* decision, not a mental one. Charlie's parents refused to come to New Zealand for the funeral, and I wondered how much the way he died played a role in their decision.

Although I cannot hope to understand the devastating grief they must have gone through, I felt a sense of relief knowing I would not have to look his mother in the eye and try to explain to her why she'd lost her beloved son in the prime of his life. As a mother myself, I knew that the only thing worse than losing a husband would be to lose a child. The shock for Charlie's parents must have been horrific, as they were completely unaware of his struggle with depression. Pangs of guilt swept through me as I thought about how I could have tried to reach out to them earlier.

I stared at my pale and drawn reflection in the mirror as I twisted off the engagement and wedding bands from my ring finger. I dropped them onto the Italian jewellery plate that Charlie had given to me on our fourteenth wedding anniversary. My throat tightened as I saw that it already contained Charlie's ring. Until then I'd forgotten that Michael had brought his ring back to me when he'd arrived for the funeral from the US the day before. I hadn't noticed that Charlie hadn't been wearing his wedding ring for a while. Michael thought I might like to have it back, as Charlie had left it at his house the last time he visited.

Remembering this made me sick. And yet, somehow, in the aftermath of his death, I knew I had to reclaim my sanity, despite all the unanswered questions. I had to stake a claim in the ground that Charlie was more than just his hanging.

Like other family members, his parents made it clear to me on the phone that they were uncomfortable with my talking so openly about his suicide. Somehow, it became an epic failure on all our parts. Being open and honest about the situation, however, seemed to me to be the only way to really separate how Charlie had died from the life he had lived.

This was easier said than done. When I told the priest from St. Benedict's parish that I wanted to at least mention his struggle with depression in the eulogy, I was told it was "not recommended."

"This is your family's service and I want you to have it the way you would like it," Father Tony reassured me, "but alluding to the facts of the situation would cause unnecessary despair for everyone."

At the time, I wondered who this "everyone" was to whom he referred, but I didn't say so. Instead, I felt myself start to disassociate from the logistics of the day. I was too exhausted and, frankly, none of it really mattered, anyway. Father Tony could work out the details himself.

That afternoon, as the winds rattled the open windows on both sides of St Benedict's, our dear friend, Gill Hodgson, sang a cappella, "You've Got A Friend." Her rich voice eased the roaring winds as it swept through the pews and filled me with a deep sense of love. Feeling as if I did have a friend at that moment, I glanced around and, for a second, was able to take in the whole scene.

The church was packed with at least 100 well-wishers from the community, who were seated or standing at the back of the church. I was taken aback by the sheer numbers who had gathered to say goodbye, and I took it as proof that we had, even if only in a small way, honoured his life as something sacred and distinct from the way he died.

One of the kindest teachers from the girls' school, Stacey, performed a traditional Maori powhiri chant as his coffin was carried from the church. Her hauntingly beautiful wail was delivered to escort Charlie's soul safely into the afterlife. The girls and I tossed stalks of fresh rosemary and lavender flowers from our garden over his coffin as it slid into the back of the hearse, and the black-suited men closed the doors in front of us, forever.

Then we watched Charlie disappear down the road.

The girls and I held hands as we walked in silence back to our car. As we did so, I wondered how on Earth I was going to pick up the pieces of my life, reclaiming my sanity and soul in the process.

*"Darkness wins by convincing us to trap it inside ourselves, instead of emptying it out."*

\- Jasmine Warga

## The Body Pays the Price

When the mind tells stories of guilt, shame, and failure, the body pays the price. According to psychologist and researcher at the University of Pennsylvania, Martin Seligman, "Depression is an emotional condition with physical consequences," and the research supports this. We now know that less than 1% of depression is due to genes, and low serotonin isn't to blame for the rest. Brain chemical imbalance is now considered to be an *effect* of depression, *not* the cause. What the experts now know is that depression is not a disease, it's a symptom, which begins in the mind and ends in the body.

There are many factors that can bring on depressive episodes, but the one we have the most control over is the way we tell our stories, and how we habitually explain and give meaning to our life's experiences. Our personal explanatory styles, as Seligman calls them, determine how susceptible we are to becoming depressed in the first place. Sometimes we favour unhelpful explanations for events, and that's okay. If we do so repeatedly and for long enough, however, our minds, bodies, and spirits begin to suffer.

Neuro-Linguistic Programming (NLP) trainer, Richard Bolstad, says, "We get good at what we practice." Depression stems from the quality of the self-talk we practice or engage in. This doesn't mean that we're to blame when the quality of our self-talk is destructive, it just means we need to practice different ways of interpreting "reality"— and different ways of telling our stories.

The plot line or events in our personal stories do not create depression, anxiety, and illness, but the characters we build into our narratives influence how upbeat or hopeless we will feel. According to intuitive healer, Caroline Myss, they're not just passive beings living in our psyches like "family portraits hanging in a dusty ancestral castle." They become either our active liberators or our ruthless prison guards.

If we have a strong helpless character playing a leading role in our tale, for example, then we are not in control of what happens to us. We play the victim. While this character may help build drama and excitement in a novel or movie, he or she can't lead us anywhere uplifting because the victim is tossed around at life's mercy and is unable to do anything about it. The same applies for any martyrs we may having lurking within our pages. The martyr is always at the mercy of others, and because of this is usually a deeply angry persona who easily morphs into a victim. These characters don't lead our stories anywhere positive.

They can't because they don't have any power; they've given it all away.

If we're able to write out the helpless or martyr characters in our stories, in particular, and replace them with ones who take more responsibility for their lives, then we change and empower ourselves in the process. If we weave hardship into learning, our lives begin to take off and cease to be pointless. We become alchemists giving birth to characters of growth and expansion. Joy then has a chance to blossom, and miracles start to occur. Our lives become rich with meaning and purpose.

There is a therapeutic process called "reframing," which reminds us that if we do not like the frame we've put around an experience, we can exchange it for another, just as we do for photos or pieces of art. This is the ultimate artistic expression we have at our disposal.

I want to remind you that you have the choice to re-write your characters, thereby transforming your life story. You have the choice to choose your own frames for both setbacks and successes. It's too late for Charlie, but I hope you still have time.

CHAPTER 6

# A New Reality

*"In three words, I can sum up everything that I have learned about life: It goes on."*

- Robert Frost

## Fire Takes the Rest

I heard the cracking, pop, pop, pop of exploding embers, but it took a few seconds to realise what was going on because I was disoriented and half-asleep from the afternoon nap I'd managed to sneak in after picking up the girls from school.

"Mommy, Mommy!" howled Francesca and Emma. "The house is on fire! Hurry!"

Jumping out of bed, I screamed down the hall to the

kitchen to find it and the laundry room filled with heavy, black smoke. Racing out the back door, I could feel the heat before I could see it. An outbuilding was fully ablaze. It was both a garage and barn and was located less than ten metres from the house. The heat from its burning walls was so intense that I couldn't breathe.

Charlie's left-hand drive Mini Cooper was engulfed in flames, too. After wrapping my sweater around my nose and mouth to keep the fierce smoke from suffocating me, I jumped into the driver's seat and quickly reversed it out of the burning building to the safety of the lawn opposite the inferno. Thankfully, he'd left the keys in the ignition. It was only afterwards that I realised the sheer scale of my stupidity: the whole backside of the car, including the petrol cap, had melted into an amorphous black and silver goo.

In an attempt to keep the flames from spreading to the house, I grabbed the garden hose and pointed it in the fire's direction, but only a light mist sprinkled out. Loud pops and hisses echoed through the air as chunks of fibrous-cement siding board exploded, throwing debris in all directions. Still clutching the hose, I ducked in and around the flying matter and tried to dodge the flames.

Then I heard the sirens. Seconds later, the Johnsonville Fire Brigade truck pulled up to the house. Someone must have dialled emergency services for us. Even before the fire crew came to a complete stop, they had one end of a massive hose in the creek at the bottom of our driveway, the other end spraying jets of pumped water in wild, high arcs. I watched as the firemen skillfully tamed the inferno on my doorstep, and almost as quickly as it had started, it was over.

Exactly four months to the day Charlie died, on 28 September 2008, all his personal belongings burned to the ground in less than thirty minutes.

Only four days earlier, I'd relocated the remainder of Charlie's things there from his office overlooking the paddock situated at the back of the house. I'd done the same with the vast majority of the photographs of the girls growing up, movies Charlie had taken of them as babies, Christmas stockings my mom had knitted, and all the camping gear we'd brought over from the US for the vacation around the South Island that had never happened.

As the firemen prepared to leave, the tall, red-haired foreman, who seemed to be in charge, told me that it had probably been caused by an electrical fault. Just like everything else on the property, the wiring was old and frayed.

The firemen packed their hoses and disappeared almost as quickly as they'd arrived. I glanced at my watch: 5:30 p.m. It wasn't even dinnertime yet. It felt surreal, and for a moment it occurred to me that maybe I'd dreamt it all up. I might have convinced myself of that possibility if it hadn't been for the new expansive view at the front of the house now that the outbuilding was gone—and the second-degree burns up my left arm.

At some point, Phil, the handyman I'd hired to help me do some yard work, sheepishly emerged from the house and confessed that he'd been charging one of Charlie's electric drills on the bench in the garage that afternoon.

## A Messenger Arrives

For days after the fire, I wandered aimlessly through the ash-covered concrete foundations that remained. Everything else was gone, including the fifty or so hay bales we'd stored under the eaves to feed the ponies.

Large holes and pockmarks from the exploding plasterboard had left their mark all over the front half of the house. All the trees and shrubs within thirty metres of the shed were covered with black, sooty grime, and the concrete foundations still smouldered under cinders, accompanied by the stench of burning debris. The fire's obnoxious odour had seeped into everything else, too, from the upholstery, curtains, and tea towels to our clothes, and even to the girls' hair. The smell seemed to linger long after I'd furiously scrubbed every daughter and soft furnishing.

Despite understanding the cause of the fire, the suddenness of the destruction rocked me to my core. For many months afterwards, I imagined "flames" in strange places. If I caught the sun's reflection out of the corner of my eye, my head spun, my heart raced, and I'd have to sit down for several minutes to keep from hyperventilating. I convinced myself that another fire could happen at any moment, and I became hyper-vigilant about unplugging appliances every night before bed.

One afternoon, as I meticulously washed down every nook and corner of the front side of the house, the whoosh of wings, belonging to an enormous kererū (New Zealand wood pigeon), grabbed my attention. Boldly, he landed on a nearby kawakawa tree (pepper tree) only a few metres away from me, at eye-level. Catching his balance after a rather abrupt crash landing, he turned to stare at me bravely, full-faced.

His protruding white chest was flanked by a small neck, head, and wings, which were covered in shiny plum and green-coloured feathers tipped with bronze. He was regal and magnificent. His appearance so close to me interrupted my spiral of self-pity and thoughts about leaving New Zealand altogether. Instead, I felt awash in peace as we gazed at each other intently.

Due to predators, such as possums and rats, and illegal hunting, kererū numbers had dropped dangerously low in New Zealand until about ten years ago, when they began to make a remarkable recovery. For this reason, this endemic wood pigeon has become a symbol of endurance. For me, he was a sign that I, too, could survive.

I will never forget his persistent presence with me that afternoon. It lingered with me long after he broke his gaze; it stayed with me even as I watched him turn to eat the cluster of yellow berries above his head on a branch covered with heart-shaped leaves.

Although my hope of returning a semblance of normalcy to the girls' lives vanished with the garage, the few moments I shared with that wood pigeon gave me renewed strength and courage to carry on. Otherwise, I may have packed up everything and returned to LA. I probably would have, if I thought we could have managed another move, and there was something to go back for.

## Finding Help for the Girls

Fears for our children are more ferocious than any other kind. My biggest one after Charlie died was its impact on the girls and what I could do to protect them. Strong anxiety grew steadily inside me until it morphed into something unrecognisable and terrifying.

Every night I lay awake trying to figure out how to save these four little lives from heartache. I replayed all the broken promises Charlie had made to them and scenarios of potential psychological damage his loss would create. If my own feelings of desertion were devastating, they were incomparable to the unrealised and nebulous feelings of abandonment I imagined my daughters would endure in the years to come. It was overwhelming.

Whenever I succumbed, my fears for my girls would leave me winded and unable to carry on with whatever I was doing at the time. My fears were like wolves on the tundra, ready to sneak up, attack, and, with their strong jaws, pierce my heart swiftly and deeply. And they always did so when I least expected them to.

One afternoon as I sat at the kitchen table helping Isabella with her homework, she told me that her school was hosting a father-daughter breakfast at the weekend and that she'd volunteered to help set up for it. At that moment, the wolves pounced and seized me, crushing my chest. I could hardly hold back my disbelief that she could help at an event that she wouldn't attend.

After several months of catastrophic thinking, I knew I had to find a way to rein in the torrent of fears I'd unleashed, but it wasn't until I was introduced to Skylight that I figured out how to do so. Skylight is one of the few organisations in New Zealand that supports families living with suicide and the loss of loved ones. With their help, I was able to start re-imagining my characters of fear into ones of strength and trust.

I enrolled in Skylight's suicide bereavement group sessions and signed the girls up for counselling sessions and art therapy. Every week for months, we went to Skylight to meet with its kind counsellors. Those sessions helped me heal and gave me the assurance that I was also doing something to help Isabella, Chiara, Emma, and Francesca.

Although I have no way of knowing what seeds of healing Skylight planted in their young minds, looking back I am not sure my girls actually did need emotional support at that time—as much as I needed them to have it. Grief, I now understand, takes years to foment and surface within our psyches, especially when we're young. We cannot force or rush losses of this magnitude. It's only now, more than a decade later, that I believe they have the maturity to begin addressing it.

What my girls did need at that time, however, was a healthy mother who could forgive herself and pick up the pieces of a broken life.

## Dealing With My Fury

To say that the months after losing Charlie were difficult is a massive understatement. I beat myself up daily with overwhelming rage and soul-destroying guilt. The self-loathing I felt when I'd spend each weekend curled up in a puddle of self-pity was unbearable. I replayed every moment of the last conversation I'd had with him in the kitchen that night - everything I'd done, every word he'd uttered, absolutely everything, and it only made things worse. If I hadn't seen this coming, how could I trust myself to keep going and make decisions now for my children? Decisions about who to trust, how to go forward, how to keep living, when it seemed inconceivable to do so.

At times, I'd pour a glass of Sauvignon Blanc (or "Sav" as they call it here) and distract myself by searching through everything Charlie had owned, including every file on his laptop. I trawled through his search engine history to try and understand what was going on inside his head. My search turned up page after page of death-by-hanging websites and instructional videos.

I found it impossible to stomach that he'd planned and researched his own demise meticulously and for at least six months beforehand. I found the small index card he'd carried around with him in his final months. Inscribed in his tiny, precise handwriting were the words: "Saint Joseph, Patron of Departing Souls, please pray for me."

I interrogated the coroner who had examined his body, as well as the witnesses who had signed his hastily-created will. I scoured old photographs to try and figure out when he had become a stranger, looking for any clues as to how this could have happened.

How could he leave us? How could he just walk out into the night and never come back? What about all the promises he made to the girls? The places he was going to take Isabella? The Italian he was going to teach Chiara? The field trip he agreed to help Emma and Francesca's teacher with? The family holiday we were going to take to the South Island?

A cold, sobering realisation swept through me. All my seeking to know and understand just kept me looking somewhere else for answers instead of facing the truth right in front of me. All the books I'd read and all the questions I asked were just elaborate and justifiable forms of distraction and denial.

Then there were the nightmares. Sleep became terrifying, and sedatives became a way of life, but only because they could help me drift off to sleep; they didn't keep me that way. For many months, I woke up in a panic at exactly the same time every morning: 3:01 am.

## I'm All Alone

The girls and I became increasingly isolated after Charlie's death as the news of his suicide spread through Wellington's northern suburbs. One afternoon a few months after the funeral, I was at a café in a mall when I overheard a woman mutter under her breath to another lady, "Oh, look, there's that American woman whose husband killed himself. I heard she burned down the barn, too."

Stunned, I stood up, ditched the sandwich I had been eating in the nearest bin, and ran to the parking lot. There I sat in my parked car long after the mall had closed, and the streets were dark: I was too numb to cry and too afraid to drive. That lady's words were daggers to my heart. Was that how people viewed us?

Aside from a few close friends, many people, particularly parents from the Pony Club, never told their children the truth about Charlie's death. As parents, our first instinct is to protect our children from the worst in the world. We rationalise that if we can keep them from reality, they'll be better off. Why on Earth would you want your children to be aware of something so horrific? Why would you want your kids to know that people can die violently by their own hand? In telling our children, doesn't it mean we are giving them an option that didn't exist before? Wouldn't this mean that our families, too, would be at risk? Was suicide contagious after all, just like what people used to believe about homosexuality?

These questions may seem like the ramblings of a crazy woman whose husband was crazy, too, but then the news media in New Zealand isn't even allowed to report on suicide for fear of so-called "copycats." Suicide gets filed in a special coroner's file and doesn't exist in this country until the coroner states officially that the only possible cause of death was obviously self-inflicted: this can take years.

And, when it comes to prevention, there's nothing to discuss because in New Zealand there is very little, and yet the high suicide rate continues to grow as it has for many years: 606 people in 2017. Suicide is the third leading cause of death among Kiwi teens.

Wouldn't the world be a better place if we could all pretend that suicide doesn't exist? I used to think so, and so did many of our new acquaintances, pulling away from us as they did, some more subtly than others. I understood their concerns at the time, but that didn't make it any less painful.

*"We're born alone, we live alone, we die alone. Only through our love and friendship can we create the illusion for the moment, that we're not alone."*

- Orson Welles

## I Overcommit

I started to question everything I did after Charlie left. I didn't trust myself. I became suspicious of my own judgments, particularly when they had to do with other people. Daily life became a challenge as I tried to keep the girls' lives as normal as possible. Getting them fed and to school every day was manageable, but getting them to Pony Club every weekend, with three horses in tow and all their riding gear intact, became impossible.

Since moving to New Zealand, I'd manically taken on

commitments that seriously overstretched me. A four-month-old border collie from Tauranga was just the start. Then there were the three grey geldings, a horse truck, twenty-four brown shaver chickens, six guinea fowl, and two peacocks from the Coromandel Peninsula; they were all essentials to the farm, I'd justified.

The sicker and more withdrawn Charlie became, the more commitments I took on. When he died I was in the process of buying another pony so that each of my girls would be able to learn to ride at the Ohariu Valley Pony Club. Looking back, it was my way of trying to outrun myself and my inability to do anything to save Charlie. My busyness was the only way I knew how to deal with the enormous sense of failure I carried.

After he died, I found it difficult to make decisions at all. Opportunities, however, continued to fall into my lap, and one of them was Tom. Twenty years my senior, he was a heavily-indebted defence lawyer originally from Australia, a good ole roll-up-your-sleeves guy: a tough, salt-of-the-earth kind of person for whom nothing was a problem. He was a relief after living with Charlie, for whom everything had become a problem. Tom also made it possible to keep going with the Pony Club, and for this I am grateful.

Tom was mostly a kind man, but he drank to ease the stress of trying to keep possession of his historic stately home in downtown Wellington. His debtors were always lurking close by. He didn't have money, and I didn't have security, so we made an unspoken exchange: he supported me physically, while I helped out financially.

The problem was that Tom wanted more from me than I could give, and as my fearful internal voice began to heal, I realised the huge mistake I'd made in getting involved with him. One evening as we sat on my front porch listening to David Gray and enjoying a pinot noir, he became agitated. I was feeling more peaceful than I had in a long time and casually told him that I didn't see a future with him, or anyone else, for that matter. I couldn't promise him anything beyond our current friendship.

Without warning, he stood up, taking the coffee table in front of us with him. Both glasses and the half-empty wine bottle abruptly flew across the deck. He then raged on for what seemed like ages about all kinds of things that I now struggle to remember. I felt dazed but came to again as he screamed, "You're worthless!" He then ran to his dilapidated Nissan 4x4 wagon and tore out of the driveway, leaving dust and confusion in his wake.

It was then I realised that I'd misread his signals. Our unspoken agreement had morphed into something scary and unpredictable. I was trying to bring safety and love in from the outside, but it wasn't to be found there.

## I Unravel Myself

Even though I knew rationally that Tom's proclamation of my worthlessness was untrue, it hit me hard and held me in its stranglehold for weeks. It also forced in me a transformation that I couldn't predict.

Only a turn of phrase, a slip-up, had caused me to tell him

the truth of my feelings that night. Why was I unable to tell him more deliberately and intentionally, even though I had felt it for some time? I now credit that moment of honesty with saving me from a deeply destructive relationship. It also brought me closer to my true self because it ushered in a new phase of self-reflection and soul-searching. It was through this turning inward that I was able to unravel myself like a huge ball of yarn, untangling the strands that gripped and held me tightly to old fears about my worthiness.

I had become a kind of shape-shifter who adapted to people and situations like a chameleon to a tree. My desire for love and acceptance was so great that I sacrificed myself to maintain the status quo and to keep people close to me, and yet it was more than acceptance I sought.

Despite the financial security it provided, my job as an account director for a New Zealand-owned advertising and public relations firm was one of the first things that needed to be unravelled. The job had become increasingly tedious after I arrived in New Zealand and, with Charlie gone, the work became meaningless. It became toxic because I no longer trusted my intuitions or skills and sitting in my office staring blankly at the screen every day drove this awareness in deeply.

I felt as if the ball of yarn that held my identity in place had been thrown over the edge of a high cliff, unravelling swiftly as it fell, and there was no one to catch me. Down I fell into the abyss of uncertainty and fear, right into the core of my being. As I fell, I unravelled all the façades I'd created to secure love and recognition from others.

I unravelled the pain and insecurity that hid under my confident exterior. I unravelled the dark stories of my past that kept me trapped in loneliness and martyrdom. I unravelled my entire universe from the inside out and from the top to the bottom. Even though there was nothing to break my fall, I eventually bottomed out into my own essence, and I was able to make friends with the pain that resided there. I was able to see how much my vitality longed to be liberated from the trap inside a dark chasm.

Finally, when there was nothing left of me but bits of dangling, frazzled threads, I was able to start transforming my lead into gold. I began a new path of self-grown love, safety, and acceptance. I trained in Neuro-Linguistic Programming and learned other practical modalities of healing, so I could shape myself more meaningfully into someone who could help others.

## Robin Williams on Being Human

Charlie met many celebrities and well-known filmmakers in Hollywood, but it was Robin Williams who made the biggest impression on him. I remember Charlie recounting the first time he laid eyes on Robin on the set of *Being Human* in Scotland.

He was absolutely blown away by Robin's sincerity and depth of compassion for everyone involved in the making of that film. Important or not, Robin didn't care. He treated every person, from the director to the kitchen hand, exactly the same, with dignity, warmth and genuine respect.

Charlie was unusually unimpressed with the celebrities who crossed his path, but he adored Robin immediately, and they went on to share a close bond based on meaningful conversation.

Since Robin's 2014 suicide, the great lengths to which his family has gone to correct the record that he died from Lewy body dementia and not depression is, I believe, a sad indictment on how society views this condition, even if that appeases the insurance provider (Lewy body dementia is covered by insurance, whereas any form of suicide is not).

Even if Lewy body is more understandable and somehow more justified, is this really the conversation we should be having? When we do, we entrench the secrecy and stigma surrounding depression and increase the pain and shame of millions of affected individuals and their families. This is not what Robin would have wanted. Through the many roles he played, as well as the person he was, he gave us a way past our human tendency to judge and assign "good" and "bad" to another person. He suspended his judgment of others, regardless of their background, life choices, or circumstances.

Fundamental to his legacy, these are the ripples that spread far and wide after he passed. Whether you knew him or not, he set a very profound example of what being human really means for all of us.

CHAPTER 7

# Writing A New Story

*"Only when we are brave enough to explore the
darkness will we discover the infinite power of our
light."*

- Brené Brown

## A Lunar Healing

I bolted upright in bed as I had done many nights before at the same time. It really wasn't a dream, I reminded myself again. My heart pounded so hard that I thought it would crack wide open and spill all over me. But instead of lying back down only to shake furiously until dawn, I got up and looked out of the bedroom window. For the first time in a month, there was no raging wind. The stars glowed brightly, which reminded me of Alaska. So, I put on my shoes and grabbed a jacket.

Shutting the mudroom door behind me, I worked my way down the dirt path alongside our chicken coop to the rear macrocarpa-lined paddock, then I climbed over the wire fence and into our neighbour's property. The walk to the pylon where the sergeant told me they'd found his body was long and steep.

Despite my panicked wake-up call, the darkness so familiar to me as a child calmed me as I climbed. It was warmer than I'd expected, too. The moon held me in its warm glow as I made my way up to the ridge of hills and Old Stage Coach Road. I love the moon in all its phases, especially when it's full. New Zealand's full moons are larger and lower in the night sky than those in North America. They feel closer and more accessible, somehow. It's as if they don't have as much room to float further away. Despite being slightly off full, this moon was more vibrant than any other I'd seen. It glowed intensely white and translucent against the jet black sky.

Under the first full moon after Charlie died, I remember wondering how it could still shine. Why would it even bother? But as I climbed that night, I no longer felt that way. This bright moon rivalled the light at midday during an Alaskan mid-winter.

As I reached the power pole where I'd journeyed in my mind on other nights when I felt too scared to get out of bed, a brief wave of dread hit me as I imagined his flailing body swinging from the third rung. The four-legged steel monstrosity was larger and more dominating here than it appeared from my kitchen window. I ducked underneath the first rung, took a deep breath, and lay down under the huge electrical structure that transferred energy from the South Island of New Zealand to Wellington and beyond.

Space enveloped me, and I felt small and insignificant under the vast sky. The weight of my petite frame rested against the earth and, strangely, I calmly took in the Southern Cross constellation overhead.

The silence and magnificence of those next moments will remain with me forever. I took in the rich, earthy smell all around me and absorbed it into my being, much as a tree or a plant sucks its nourishment from the soil. Just as I'd done in the snow as a child, I made "angels" with my arms and legs in the damp, cool grass.

As I did so, all the memories of my life with Charlie flashed through my mind, and I watched them as if I were watching a movie of my life—no longer feeling the need to question it. A powerful sense of forgiveness, gratitude, and peace washed over me, and the light of the stars filled and surrounded me, too. For the first time since I'd made friends with the dark as a seven-year-old, I felt truly alive there in that most unlikely place.

Then, with total abandon, I suddenly howled into the night air. My voice echoed up and over the pylon and down across Ohariu Valley and finally to disappear into infinity. Unlike the high-pitched, short bursts of "woo, woo, woo" the LA coyotes made at night, I howled as an Alaskan timber wolf—wild, deep, guttural wails of confidence, space, and freedom.

# A Turning Point

As I worked my way back down the hill to the house, the stars reminded me of the Northern Lights that kept me company as a child. Every northern culture has legends about the Aurora, and one Inuit myth describes these dancing lights as torches in the hands of spirits who are escorting the souls of the dead over the abyss at the edge of the world.

My third-grade teacher, who was half-Athabaskan Eskimo told me this story and said that it was much more than just a myth. She knew without a shadow of a doubt that her ancestors were those lights, celebrating because they'd been liberated from their Earthly suffering. She would always see them sky dancing, she told me.

Taking in the stars that night, I knew they'd set Charlie free, too. I also knew he loved me, after all, and that the love I longed for when I was with him, and that of the other men in my dreams, was not this kind of love.

The love I had now was unconditional, expansive and permanent, and did not rely on one man's capacity to give it to me based on his mental wellbeing, or anything else so inconstant. This love came from deep inside me and, at the same time, somewhere else entirely. It had no bounds or limitations and was big enough to hold all of me: my personality with its flavours and faults, as well as my true self.

The sun began to rise as I continued my descent of the hill, and I didn't resent it any more for doing so. As I turned my face towards its warm rays, I breathed in a deep sense of peace. For the first time since moving to New Zealand, I felt at home.

That night was a turning point for me at every level. The fear and rage that had closed in on me were driven back with that howl. Since then, when they threaten to sneak back in, usually on a birthday or significant anniversary, the strength of this memory remains, and I am flooded with enormous love, gratitude, and appreciation for myself and all living things.

> *"Out of suffering have emerged the strongest souls;*
> *the most massive characters are seared with scars."*

> - Khalil Gibran

## Carving Our Bowls

A therapist I'd seen after Charlie died, Sally, told me that I was one of the luckiest people she had ever met. Her words shocked me.

She explained that the more intense our suffering the deeper we carve our "bowls," and I now had a deeply-carved bowl. Cupping her hands to show me, she said that a carved bowl gives depth to our souls and compassion to our hearts.

She was right; it actually works like this, even if we haven't learned or practiced viewing our struggles in this way. All the people I've ever admired had deeply-carved bowls.

Now I could see it for what it was: a sacred gift. My bowl is bursting over, and for the first time in my life, I have love to give away, and I am immensely grateful. I wake up every day knowing what a privilege it is to support people as they work through their own, or a loved one's, inner darkness. I know this because if we embrace it, we can transform ourselves and find a joy we never knew existed.

When Charlie died, the entire world came to an end. Not just my world, but the whole universe ceased to exist. Then, to my utter surprise, it did not end, and this is one of my most profound lessons.

Focusing on this simple truth, I can now celebrate Charlie's life, along with my family's loss. I am grateful to him as one of my best teachers.

In facing my own darkness head on, I really have carved my bowl, and it is beautiful.

I now know that Charlie was right: I was better off without him, but not for the reasons he'd said.

C H A P T E R  8

# Losing Mom and Finding Myself

*"Between stimulus and response there is a space. In that space is our power to choose our response. In our response lies our growth and our freedom."*

- Viktor Frankl, MAN'S SEARCH FOR MEANING

## A Powerful Choice

Society apportions blame differently for physical and mental illness, and yet all disease is emotional, physical, and spiritual, all at the same time. If we could approach disease as the inner darkness trying to break free in physical form, we wouldn't seek solutions in isolation, nor would we be surprised when an imbalance in one area of our lives—our emotions—has physical implications. The mind-body experts have explained this phenomenon and have given us a way to understand the interconnectedness of our health: so why do we resist?

Why is someone more at fault when he or she succumbs to depression, but not to cancer? Why is it more acceptable to say a person died from Parkinson's disease or dementia, for example, even if the result is the same–death?

Why is it so damning to say someone killed himself from chronic, long-term depression? Is it because, deep down, we think of disease as something that just happens to us, something over which we have no control? To commit suicide, we must do so with our own hands, our own intention, our own will power, and this leads us directly to choice.

But in reality, we all have the choice to live or die and are making this choice in every moment of our lives, whether or not we realise it. We choose the stories we tell and then repeat them. We interpret the events that happen to us as either failures or setbacks, or we decide they'll be learnings and growth. Of all the choices we make in our lives, this one is the most powerful.

Classifying people as "mentally ill" is destructive. It may validate feelings and provide some comfort to families struggling to support them, but, ultimately, it only reinforces the hardened core of dysfunction, which is the individual's own dark inner voice.

If we could make more room for a greater variety of psychological "abnormalities" within our collective hearts, this increased acceptance, and the space it creates to fearlessly face our own imperfections and setbacks, might help heal this rapidly-growing modern epidemic.

As human beings, we *all* need psychological support at times. We also long for straight-forward, black and white answers to personal challenges and life's difficulties. Unfortunately, there are no such answers when it comes to suicide. It seems so wrong on so many levels yet thinking of it in this way only hardens our fears and isolates those suffering and those left behind.

*"People are like stained-glass windows. They sparkle and shine when the sun is out, but when the darkness sets in their true beauty is revealed only if there is light from within."*

- Elisabeth Kübler-Ross

## A Promise to Myself

Sadie threw her arms around me as I entered Mom's cabin. God, I was happy to see my sister! I studied her face closely. Despite her cool as a cucumber demeanour, her eyes flashed a surge of panic.

Making our way down the hallway, I began to feel claustrophobic as we drew closer to Mom's open-plan kitchen/dining room. The drone of her oxygen tank with its monotonous hissing and ticks greeted me before she did.

In the middle of the room, where the dining table had been, Mom was lying on a rollaway hospital bed with metal bars along each side. Her large frame was covered only by a blue calico nightshirt. Band Aids decorated her forearms.

Feeling light-headed, I tried to take in the long, clear tubes that connected her nose to the stainless steel tank on the floor beside the bed. I'm not sure what I expected, but this wasn't it. I knew she was really sick, but I still couldn't believe this was my mom. It was Thanksgiving, after all. She should have been standing in the kitchen preparing pumpkin pies.

As I moved closer, she peered at me intensely. Set against a pale, bloated face, her dark eyes were unfamiliar. So, too, were the thin, blue lips which curled upwards to acknowledge me.

"Hi, Mom," I said, placing a kiss on her forehead.

A smile forced its way out from under her suffering, bringing tears to her eyes. The intensity and ferociousness that had terrified me as a child seemed incomprehensible at that moment. I'd always been intimidated by her impulsive outbursts, but seeing her lying there, I wondered if I'd imagined it all. Maybe this, too, was just a story I'd created, which would, like all stories, eventually come to an end.

Sadie emerged from behind the refrigerator door with a bottle of chardonnay. She poured four glasses of wine, and we toasted Mom and Thanksgiving. We then raised our glasses to Jim, who was looking exhausted and much older than I remembered. Because we all lived so far away, it was my stepfather who'd made it possible for her to stay at home by caring for her around the clock.

After a short catch up, Mom drifted off to sleep. The rest of us moved to the adjacent lounge, where I asked about her medication.

"Morphine," Sadie said. "For pain... and to help relax her airways, so she can breathe more easily."

"That's strong stuff," I replied. "Is it really necessary? She seems like a bit of a zombie."

"Yes, I know," Jim blurted, defensively, "but the doctor says she's on the right dosage and can't cope without it."

As the oxygen machine continued its merciless whir in the next room, I glanced at my sister.

"Can't we reduce it somewhat just while we're here?" I asked, not wanting to undermine Jim's authority.

A loud pounding on the front door interrupted our conversation. Within seconds, a rather plump middle-aged woman carrying a large black bag was standing at the door of the lounge. Looking serious and officious, she introduced herself. "I'm Kathleen with Hospice."

Mom was fast asleep, with a line of foamy drool sliding down from the left corner of her mouth. Kathleen pulled a tissue out of her pocket and casually wiped her chin. Then she began checking Mom's blood pressure and oxygen levels. After adjusting her bedsheets, Kathleen checked the incontinence pad upon which mom was lying.

"I'm putting in a catheter now," she announced. "Glenda

isn't able to control her bladder any longer. This will make it more comfortable for everyone," she reassured.

Mom stirred slightly as Kathleen said this. I approached the bed and took her hand in one of mine and, with the other, I pushed a long strand of grey fringe away from her face. How could she be the same fiercely independent woman I'd felt incarcerated by as a child? I thought.

As Kathleen searched her bag for the equipment, Mom opened her eyes. "Make sure you don't overcook the turkey," she suddenly whispered. Kathleen then raised Mom's nightdress to insert the tube.

"Don't worry about the bird," I reassured her, catching my breath. "We're experts. Remember, you taught us well. Nobody makes Thanksgiving turkey as well as you do. Besides, you'll make sure we're doing it right," I teased.

Sadie chimed in from across the room and began reciting everything we planned to prepare the next day: sausage and cranberry stuffing, roast garlic mashed potatoes, giblet gravy, sautéed Swiss chard with currants, and Mom's famous pumpkin pie with brandy whipped cream for dessert.

When I saw Mom wince, I knew the catheter had reached its destination. Sadie and I helped change Mom's underpad to a dry one. Then Kathleen removed her plastic gloves and packed her things, and we followed her to the front door.

"Glenda is lucky you are here with her for Thanksgiving,"

she started. "I've worked in Hospice for 30 years now, and what I've noticed is that people get this particular smell right before they die. Your mom smells like that now."

Then, abruptly, Kathleen turned and left the house.

Stunned, I turned to Sadie.

"That's crazy! Mom's not well, but she's not that bad."

Sadie nodded almost imperceptibly, and we turned in for the night.

But I couldn't stop thinking about what Kathleen had said, and not long afterwards I started throwing up; then came diarrhoea. Hour after hour, my stomach turned itself inside out, and I violently propelled everything from my body. I spent much of the night in Mom's bathroom until I couldn't any more, and my abdomen hurt so badly I could hardly sit up.

By morning, however, I felt better. As quickly as it had arrived, it stopped. And although I felt weak, the turkey Sadie had put in the oven earlier smelled amazing. I was relieved to see that Mom was more alert, too.

"Happy Thanksgiving, Mom," I said, kissing her cheek. "It's your favourite day of the year." She smiled back at me with a bit of colour to her cheeks.

"Don't forget to put the garlic in before you boil the potatoes," she instructed in a raspy, weak voice. It was such a relief to hear her kitchen orders once again.

We worked all morning preparing the other Thanksgiving dishes, stopping only to raise a toast of bubbles to Mom and ask for culinary advice. It was almost like old times. But Mom was more hands-off than usual. Jim, and Sadie's husband, Josh, watched football on TV in the next room, and we chatted about the kids, our jobs and anything else we could think of, including past Thanksgiving recipe debacles.

"How about the year you decided to deep fry the turkey, Mom?" Sadie reminisced when there was about an hour to go before lunch. "Remember? You hired that enormous deep fat fryer, and Jim stoked it up under a wood fire in the back yard? If it hadn't been for the snow, you would have burnt the house down!"

Sadie and I laughed as we continued chopping the onions and tossed Swiss chard into the skillet.

Suddenly, I put down my wooden spoon and turned to look at Mom. The blood had drained from her face, and she was foaming at the mouth. I rushed to wipe the corner of her lips with the tea towel I'd grabbed en route. She was drawn and lifeless. We gathered around and held her close. I rubbed her shoulders and ran my fingers gently through her hair.

Silently, she slipped away from us. Right there in the middle of preparing the Thanksgiving feast, less than a foot away from the roasting turkey, Mom died.

I laid my head against her chest to see if I could feel her heartbeat. But I knew she was gone. Big, fat tears carrying

years of sadness and regret rolled down my face and onto
her body. I regretted the times I couldn't bring myself to
tell her how much I loved her, the times when I had held
her at arm's length, and all the times I judged her unfairly.

Then, rays of soft winter sunshine began pouring
through the stained glass kitchen window that Mom had
made many years before. The tender mother and child
scene coloured the light and they began to glow. Red, green,
yellow and orange hues illuminated Mom's forehead like
the Northern Lights, which sometimes danced on the snow.
For a moment that felt like an eternity, I watched her being
cradled in the sun's embrace.

Just like that, she was gone. The sun retracted its light,
and Jim disconnected the oxygen tank and called Hospice.

There was no way we could have planned it, but it was
perfect that way. Mom died with my sister and I at her
side. If she could have held on for another hour, she would
have enjoyed her last Thanksgiving meal, or at least told
us what we could have done to improve it. But then again,
the preparation had always been her favourite part.

After putting away the Thanksgiving dinner that nobody
ate, a raw numbness enveloped me. She wouldn't suffer
any longer, and I was grateful I had got there on time. It
would have been hard to forgive myself if I hadn't.

On 25 November 2010, I made a promise to myself. I
wouldn't carry on with my habitually dark thinking styles.
I would learn new ways of making sense of my life and new
ways of telling my old story.

# Beating My Addiction

Despite having promised myself I would stop taking antidepressants when the twins turned a year old, I had not been able to do so. That's because they're incredibly addictive, which wasn't something my doctor told me when he prescribed them to me in the first place.

Even though my morning 20 mg of fluoxetine (a cheaper, generic form of Prozac) helped me cope with difficult times, as soon as I tried to stop taking them I'd start crying uncontrollably. My sleep became disrupted, too, which sent me down into a spiral of fatigue and exhaustion.

The first time I tried, I went cold turkey. I became a crying, crumpled mess and spent the weekend curled up in a ball on the living room floor, listening to Charlie's favourite music. After that, I tried at least half a dozen times to reduce my dosage and eliminate them gradually by breaking the white, spherical tablets in half. The crying and lack of sleep weren't as bad this way, but after about three weeks, my friends would notice something was wrong and would tell me so.

My friend, Melissa, in particular, had an uncanny way of knowing and a certain way of checking in with me each time. I can still see her raised left eyebrow which ushered in the look that told me she knew I'd gone off them. She wouldn't say a word, but she'd give me a sideways school mistress glance that spoke volumes. The next morning, and sometimes even sooner, my daily pharmaceutical ritual would resume, and I'd tell myself that I needed them more than I'd thought. A sense of relief accompanied each reversal, but it paled in comparison to every defeat.

Eventually, I was only able to get off them with the help of my doctor and increasingly smaller and, eventually, infinitesimal doses spread over the course of a year. Through that process, I endured months of emotional wobbles, but with the help of spiritual therapy, meditation, and an alcohol-free and raw foods diet, I finally managed to shake the monkey off my back.

As bad as the withdrawal from antidepressants was, the fact that they'd kept me from dealing with my inner darkness earlier, and more decisively, was–by far–their worst side effect. What I have come to understand is that in denial we make ourselves sick. It is only through tremendous courage and sobering honesty that we are able to free ourselves from depression's dark chains.

Antidepressants deaden our vitality, which is sacred but not always easy to live with. Reaching for a pill when we feel down or anxious may seem like a good idea at the time–and it can be if we really are unable to cope–but it also makes it too easy to ignore the promptings of our true selves. Antidepressants numb our inner turmoil, and, in taking the edge off, we are less likely to find the courage and strength to face our uncomfortable inner demons, which will never truly go away if we don't make room for them. It's only when we face our darkness and befriend it that we can unlock its gifts.

Antidepressants make it easier to slip back into living our lives on autopilot, and it's in this place that we habitually re-tell the same old worn out stories, instead of re-inventing ourselves through the process of writing new and more uplifting ones.

*"We cannot change anything unless we accept it."*

- Carl Jung


# A Prize for Me, Too

I almost didn't make it. Five minutes after the prize-giving was scheduled to start, I ran out of the door and sprinted three blocks to Baradene College of the Sacred Heart's auditorium, where I was ushered upstairs to the balcony overlooking the stage. Trying hard to contain my heaving chest, I climbed over a row of more punctual parents and took the last remaining seat between two Polynesian families.

I noticed that everyone was seated in family groups or pairs, and I was definitely the only single parent. Maybe they were just friends, I said to myself. Maybe they were uncles, aunts, and cousins. Nevertheless, I stood out–a familiar feeling for me since moving to New Zealand nine years earlier. It was at times like this that I missed Charlie the most. Our beautiful, amazing daughter, Chiara, was graduating from high school and preparing to study law and political science at Otago University in Dunedin the following year. A sadness gripped my chest like a vice. Once again, he'd miss a family milestone.

He'd missed so much: Isabella's graduation from

university, Francesca's first-place prize in a creative writing competition, and Emma's "Most Valuable Player" award for her field hockey team. Moments parents shared and celebrated together.

As the Dean started to present the university entrance scholarships, I secretly hoped it wouldn't take too long. My mind wandered back home to where I'd left the twins sitting at the kitchen table.

"...Scholarships for the University of Auckland, Victoria University, University of Otago, are blah, blah, blah, blah..." One by one, the girls—dressed in black and gold pinstriped blazers, with gold ties, and excessively long black skirts—trundled across the stage to collect their certificates. Aside from their heads, necks and knuckles, they were covered in dark, heavy fabric; this was Catholic school, after all.

Then I heard it... "Blah, blah, blah, Chiara Ireland." Oh, wow! That's my girl! My maternal pride kicked in full force as I watched her petite frame and familiar stride cross the stage to shake hands with the Baradene College elite. She received scholarships to every major university in the country, and I hadn't even realised she'd applied!

I didn't hear the remaining announcements because the intense wave of pride that filled my chest overtook my mental capacities for a while. I was lost in the sweet memory of my two-year-old girl dressed in her red and white polka-dotted Minnie Mouse frock. So happy and easy going, and yet so fiercely independent at the same time. She'd always done well at school, but she applied herself, too.

Of all my girls, I worried the most about Chiara after Charlie died. I couldn't help but feel relieved to see her excel, despite the enormous pain she carried, and the anger she sometimes expressed, particularly towards me.

I can't claim credit for any of it, of course, and yet it somehow signalled we'd both made it, despite the odds. We were still here and moving forward. We hadn't given up.

Following the keynote address from an alumna who'd built a successful global landscaping company, the faculty heads of departments awarded girls who stood out in each area of study. Having tasted the sweet nectar of maternal pride once already, I was more alert for the duration of the announcements. One by one, they read off the names of the girls who excelled in science, maths, English, Te Reo Maori, and religious education.

Chiara received first in Classical Studies for her year. Weeks before, I'd noticed a copy of Homer's *Iliad and Odyssey* on her bedside table. There she was again, walking across the stage with her head held high. "That's my Chiara!" I wanted to shout at the top of my lungs. With my heart the size of a watermelon in mid-summer, I squirmed in my seat a bit too energetically and received a sideways glance from the woman seated next to me.

Then I heard it, the announcement that still brings a song to my heart and a chuckle to my throat: "The 2016 winner of Baradene College of the Sacred Heart's Cor

Unum Award for Compassion and Kindness to Others is... Chiara Ireland!"

I took in a huge suck of breath as I glanced at the lady next to me. "Really?" I whispered under my breath. "Chiara receiving an award for compassion and care for others?"

Chiara is an amazing and kind young woman, yet for her to receive the top award for character and concern for others was still incredible. After the twins were born, she seemed to fight hard for her place in the family and, once Charlie was gone, she developed an edge to her that I found difficult to connect with. Somehow, she was more reticent to express her feelings after he was gone.

I'd missed many dance and debate performances over the years because she "forgot" to tell me about them. She hadn't even insisted that I come to this prize-giving. She nonchalantly mentioned it a week or so earlier, saying, "You can come if you want to, Mom."

In a way, I lost part of Chiara, too, when Charlie died. I lost her younger, more carefree self. She stopped turning to me for support as often as she once had, probably to protect us both. I know that she didn't want to add to the load she saw me carry.

As I strolled home in the dark after the awards ceremony, I thought of everything Charlie had missed over the years. This was near the top of that list, for sure, but in some small way, I was lighter this time. He walked with me, and I breathed this realisation into me with the sweet night air.

Just then I glanced ahead at the horizon. In front of me, set against a palette of dark blue, was a brilliant pale-yellow full moon floating gently above the trees, seemingly suspended in the air by invisible strings. These same "strings" carry my maternal pride and will keep my girls connected to me forever.

Knowing that he was still with us, I felt as expansive as the universe; the love and memories he left behind still existed somewhere in eternity beyond all understanding.

At least for a night, I felt successful. It was okay to feel proud, despite the fact that I knew Chiara's accolades were all her own. Still, all those hugs I gave, wet towels I picked up off the bedroom floor, school sandwiches I'd made, the music and tennis lessons for which I'd scraped together the funds, and all the times I'd bitten my tongue during emotional outbursts were something, at least. I'd got her this far, along with her three sisters, despite the times when I really didn't think I had the strength to do so.

At that moment, I became aware that my heart had cried, but it didn't break, and I wouldn't have missed it for the world.

## A Howl for Humanity

As crazy as it sounds, I still howl at the moon, as I did sprawled out under that pylon. I blurt out great howls of unconditional love and forgiveness for Charlie, and compassion for myself for the part I played. I howl for my mother, who endured her own battle with depression, and I howl for myself and everything I now have to give others living half-lives in darkness.

I howl for the suffering of the world, and the incredible love I now have for every living being on Earth.

I howl for the personal lies and the stories we sometimes tell, for the mental bars we use to imprison ourselves, and for the judgments we have about what's healthy and so-called "normal."

I also howl for the people who believe in societies' collective lies.

I howl for the narrow and restrictive beliefs we have about what is supposedly acceptable, and for how difficult it can be to really live by the "promptings of our true selves," wherever they lead us.

I ask you to join me in these howls because the consequences of believing, and in living these dark stories are fatal, but even more importantly, they are soul destroying.

Because...

**It's a lie to believe you are not good enough.**

**It's a lie to believe you are not worthy.**

**It's a lie to believe that you should be something or someone you are not.**

**It's a lie to believe you have failed... at anything.**

## My Search Stops

I've told you some of my story in these pages. I long to tell you why it happened in the first place. Why did such an amazing man with so much talent and support from a loving family die at the mercy of his own hands when he was only forty-six?

I now realise that even if I look under every stone, visit every city, every country, every forest, every hidden corner of this incredible planet, I still wouldn't find the answer. I could scan the heavens and talk to every star, and I still wouldn't know. I could interview every expert and absorb every research paper and still not understand why Charlie took his own life.

This profound truth has left me with only these things to do: let go of trying to understand it; release my need to know and explain it and free myself from the unrelenting search to make sense of suicide, because some things are inexplicable.

My devastation can only be understood by my heart, not my head. Whenever there is a loss, however, our first inclination is to try and reason with it when, in fact, losing the people we love in any capacity is the most unreasonable thing that can ever happen. We cannot find logical answers as to why it took place any more than we can explain why the sun rises or the moon shines.

This does not mean we don't try to help when and where we can, but we must allow ourselves to let go when holding on only spreads the suffering. In doing so, we release ourselves from the pain and guilt, and we set them free, too.

I have given Charlie back to the Universe to be reabsorbed into the infinite where he belongs. I continue to hold with both hands the ambiguity of losing him in all its shades of grey and give it up to the sky like doves returning home. The wings of those doves carry messages, important ones, with practical learnings about how we can change our life stories to ones filled with great love and understanding.

## I Rewrite My Ending

I don't know all the answers to depression or suicide, but I do have a few, and they are powerful. I know what helps and what worsens this human condition. And I am lucky to be able to share what I experienced as a child, living with Charlie, and helping people recover and thrive.

I know that depression fills us with hopelessness over hope, resignation over curiosity, and self-blame over self-love. It saps us of our essence and the very life force needed to function and fulfil our purpose on Earth. Depression is also a cry for meaning, speaking persistently and honestly about our spiritual, as well as our emotional, wellbeing. If we do not fill this gap in our lives and live by the promptings of our true selves, then the darkness waiting in the wings may move in and try to fill it for us. And fill it, it will–but not with what we want.

Back in 1946, psychologist and Holocaust survivor, Viktor Frankl, reflected in Man's Search For Meaning that we needed to stop asking "What is the meaning of life, and instead think of ourselves as being questioned by life– daily and hourly." When we ask what life wants from us, and, at the same time, explore what we desire from life, this two-way conversation provides an expansive road- map for living in a divine and sacred way. It allows us to co-create with something greater than ourselves to build hope and mental resilience, qualities that were needed as much during WWII as they are today, in our materialistic, secular and, often, isolated modern lives.

I realise now that I have an obligation to share what few answers I have with those who are lost, confused and at the mercy of depression's grip. I'm driven to help people battling their way through dark and meaningless lives. In starting this work I had a choice: I could continue in uncer- tainty or I could reach out to others who may benefit from my experience. I could help people find the strength to rewrite their personal "stories" by making different choices than the ones they practiced growing up.

I've re-written my story in this way, and it's given me a deep sense of knowing that, regardless of what we look like, how smart we are, how we behave, what we struggle with, or where we come from, we are all perfect exactly as we are.

My coaching practice is grounded on radical acceptance, which creates space to experience an inner divinity that is undervalued in our fast-paced, modern lives. As I shine light into dark places, I teach people how to look at and accept their original stories, and then work to transform them into tales of empowerment and joy.

I lean in and listen closely to people as they struggle and, in doing so, I help them hold their condition (or that of a loved one) more gently and with greater room for abnormality and darkness.

Just as I listened to the wolves in Alaska, I hear them with my whole heart and being. Because I know that when I do this, miracles happen. Often for the first time, people can feel the hope and love all around them. In moving towards, not away from, our darkness, we re-write depressive episodes, and they carve our bowls.

I have learned many things from losing Charlie, but one of the most significant is that I am no longer afraid of the dark, in any form. The more fully I face it and soak it in, the brighter my world seems to get. The less resistance I experience, the more loving and quieter my inner voice becomes. And it's from this still place that I can joyfully re-write my story, celebrating both my life and Charlie's.

*"In the new reality, all are born into a story. It is a story which everyone creates and which everyone lives, with darkness or with light, in freedom."*

- Ben Okri, THE FREEDOM ARTIST

*Digging the house out in Fairbanks, Alaska*
*Molly and her mom (1970)*

*After the snow melts,*
*Molly with her little brother,*
*Chuck, Alaska (1972)*

*Charlie and bear, Hertfordshire, UK (1964)*

*Charlie at Manchester University, UK (1980)*

*Charlie with Mike Ellis, Princess Diana,*
*Prince Harry and Prince William,*
*Pinewood Studios (1992)*

*Robin Williams, on the set of*
*Being Human (1992)*

*Charlie and Chiara in Monterey, CA (1999)*

*Emma and Francesca in Sherman Oaks, CA (2001)*

*Francesca, Emma and "Despereaux"*
*the hamster (2003)*

*Off to school (from left to right):*
*Isabella, Francesca, Chiara and Emma in*
*Topanga, CA (2006)*

*Charlie climbing Alpe d'Huez (2007)*

*The Ireland girls (left to right):*
*Francesca, Emma, Chiara and Isabella*
*in Ngaio, Wellington (2007)*

*Charlie and his girls exploring Venice, Italy (2007)*

*The Ireland girls with "Willie" the pony in Ohariu Valley, Wellington (2008)*

Coming soon by
Molly Ireland:

To learn more visit:
www.beyondthecourse.co.nz

Made in the USA
San Bernardino, CA
01 March 2020

65210727R00100